BROKEN PROMISES

How insurers put Profits over Promises

DAVID SKIPTON

CPCU, PCLA, LPCS, SPPA, AIC,AINS

President/Executive General Adjuster, for
SKIPTON claims management

Broken Promises
Copyright © 2025 by David Skipton

ISBN: 979-8894791906 (hc)
ISBN: 979-8894791883 (sc)
ISBN: 979-8894791890 (e)

The Reading Glass Books
1-888-420-3050
www.readingglassbooks.com
fulfillment@readingglassbooks.com

Table of Contents

Dedication

I want to dedicate this work to my mentor, my long-time business partner and my friend, Mr. Victor Dennis Beard. E.G.A. (Executive General Adjuster), deceased. Victor was the most passionate, brilliant and successful claims adjuster I have ever known. Victor gave me the highest standards to measure success and constantly challenged me to think through each coverage argument and claim situation to find the winning strategy for our clients. It was a joy to watch the "Master" command the utmost respect from so many adversarial companies and their battalions of attorneys. They say that the greatest gift one can bestow upon another is the gift of knowledge; I thank you Victor for your generous gift and I miss you.

David Skipton

Foreword

August 24, 2015

If you've suffered an insured loss to your business or home, *you need to read this book*! I have a personal experience with a multi-million dollar commercial claim that changed my life, as will the journey upon which you are about to embark. Whether your claim is large or small, the good news is that as an informed consumer of the insurance product you've purchased, the knowledge gained in this book will give you a great advantage in obtaining maximum legitimate dollars that you're owed. The bad news is that the adjuster (or adjusters) assigned by the insurance company, handles claims like yours every day, and, while a personal experience for you, it is just everyday business for the adjuster and insuror.

This book is full of actual examples encountered by Skipton Associates in the preparation of claims for their clients. I know they are true, accurate, and very common. As a public adjuster for 30 years, like Dave Skipton, I've experienced all these examples. Truth be known, I see new games played by carriers on almost every new major claim. Their armies of lawyers, "experts", trainers and lobbyists continue to create new obstacles for your financial recovery while you attempt to use the product that's cost you thousands of dollars over time to purchase.

Here's the Reader's Digest of my story and how it changed by life: In 1985, I had a very successful career as a commercial real estate broker and developer. I was also on my fraternity house board. In late October, an arsonist burned six fraternity houses along the Colorado Front Range, and mine was one of them. My board assigned me to handle the insurance claims. Two claims, because after the arson fire, the house was vacated and boarded up, and someone broke in and lit it up again! I'd had an auto claim in the past, but no other insurance experience. Neither had anyone else on the board, so my real estate and construction experience was the best we had. We were underinsured, but the two fires created the opportunity to collect on the same policy twice. The company adjuster was polite, and seemed like a nice guy. So were the public adjusters that solicited my business to prepare the claim for the fraternity.

Needless to say, I was conflicted. Should I allow the insuror to prepare my claim, or hire a PA? I consulted with my board. When I asked our general counsel, he said "if they don't pay what they owe, we'll sue them". How would I know what they owed? When I asked my fraternity brother insurance broker, he said, "before you hire a PA, let them make an offer". Why would I let them make an offer and try to negotiate UP from there? I decided to ask the nice, professional insurance company adjuster. He said "PA's will just take your money; I will pay you every penny I owe". That answer alone made no sense to me. Nor did my board. I interviewed three PA's, checked their references, and hired one. In retrospect, it was one of the best decisions I'd ever made (except marrying my wife of 40 years). There is no way I could have collected as much as the PA did. His knowledge of customary adjusting practices (which the company adjuster knew by heart), insurance law, and some obscure policy benefits (which the adjuster never told me existed) allowed this to transpire. I shadowed the PA while he worked, fell in love with the business, and bought his company after he collected almost twice the policy limits!

That was then; this year, I was selected by my peers as president of the National Association of Public Insurance adjusters, and Dave Skipton is one of my most trusted colleagues. Dave has written a hard hitting expose and excellent resource to help you understand your options and guide you in making good choices as you pursue the product you paid hard earned premiums for. Please read your insurance policy, then read it again. Ask questions of your "nice" adjuster, and if (or when) you get to the end of your rope, and are too frustrated to go on, interview a public adjuster. A good one will counsel you on your options, and be interviewing you as much as you're interviewing them to see if it's a good fit for both. Only *you* get to decide if retaining a PA is a good choice, or if you wish to go it on your own.

If you've suffered an insured loss to your business or home, ***you need to read this book!***

My career as a public adjuster started with a personal experience on a multi-million dollar commercial claim that changed my life, as will the journey upon which you are about to embark. Whether your claim is large or small, the good news is that as an informed consumer of the insurance product you've purchased, the knowledge gained through this book will give you a great advantage in obtaining the fair settlement that you are owed. The bad news is that the adjuster assigned by the insurance company, handles claims like yours every day, and, while a personal experience for you, it is just everyday business for the adjuster and insurance company.

This book is full of actual examples encountered by Dave Skipton in the preparation of claims for their clients. I know they are true, accurate, and very common, as I have worked as a public adjuster for 30 years, and like Dave Skipton, I've experienced all these examples.

This year, I was selected by my peers as president of the National Association of Public Insurance Adjusters (NAPIA). Dave Skipton is one of my most trusted colleagues. He has written a hard hitting expose' and excellent resource to help consumers understand their options after a loss and guide them in making good choices as they pursue the fair claim settlement that they paid their hard earned premiums for.

R. Scott deLuise, CPPA, SPPA, CCIM

INTRODUCTION

This book is a revision to **The Claims Game** and is intended to provide consumers with an easy-to-understand overview of how the insurance claims process works in today's profit hungry world of insurance. Insurance companies have discovered a new source of revenues and it comes directly from the pockets of their most vulnerable customers. This new revenue source is from claims payments and if you have a claim, you are likely to be one of their unwitting victims.

If you have just recently had a loss, you should jump to the Appendixes at the back of this book and read them first. These Appendixes are designed to provide you with important information to protect yourself from predatory claims handling practices.

The aftermath of a serious loss event and the uncertainty that it brings can be extremely unsettling. Few people will ever deal with a major property claim and most are not well-equipped to deal with the claims process. As such, most of them are forced to rely upon the guidance and goodwill of their insurance company to assist them in their recovery. Unfortunately, all too often, the guidance provided is not so much aimed at the customer's recovery as it is at minimizing the cost of the claim to the insurance company.

This book will not train you to adjust your own claim. It takes years of training and a much more extensive curriculum than is practical in one book. But the improper claims practices described in this book will help you identify wrongdoing and alert you about what to look for to assure that you are being dealt with fairly by your insurance company. Knowing how the game is played can empower the consumer to take actions to protect their interests. Understanding the claims game can provide a measure of clarity in the uncertain world of those who have suffered a catastrophic loss. It can also be your first step to a proper and fair recovery.

We have tried to make this book as interesting as possible, but let's be honest, insurance is not the most interesting subject unless you have just had a major loss. Insurance claims can be highly complex, and, like fingerprints, each claim has its own unique characteristics.

This book should serve as a guide to help you navigate the claims process and more effectively work with your insurance company on more equal ground.

Chapter One

"Not Your Daddy's Insurance Company"

Bill and Ruth just returned home to Sun City, Arizona after a few weeks visiting friends and family in Kansas. As they pulled into the driveway, they noticed water pouring out from under the garage door and running down the driveway. After 17 hours on the road, this was the last thing they needed.

Upon opening the garage door, their worst fears were confirmed as their home was several inches deep in water. This was no ordinary water leak; this was a high-pressure line that must have gone on for days as the water damages stretched from one end of their beautiful home to the other. This was their Arizona retirement home that they had dreamed of for years and it was nearly perfect, situated on a Sun City golf course in a gorgeous retirement community. Bill had taken pride in perfecting every detail to entertain guests, with an impressive outdoor bar that even included draft beer. He didn't miss a thing in creating his dream home.

Bill grew up dirt poor as a child, but through hard work and perseverance, he worked his way up the corporate ladder at Ford Motor Company, rising from doing odd jobs in the parts department to eventually becoming a Vice-President. Bill was truly a self-made man who prided himself in having the best, be it his perfectly maintained cars or the dozens of exotic designer shoes he had purchased. These things and his home were a symbol of a life that was both hard-earned and well-deserved.

But Bill and Ruth's dream was now threatened by an unforeseen water pipe break that wreaked destruction upon their home and all of their belongings. Bill's first reaction was to call his insurance agent, who politely gave him the name of an emergency services company that specializes in water extractions. Then, Bill remembered that an old friend from Ford had gone to work recently in the insurance claims business, so his next call was to his friend for advice on how to handle this situation.

Bill's friend had recently come to work in the marketing department of our firm in our Dallas, Texas office. He explained to Bill how we represent the policyholder's interests in settling insurance claims for a small fee. Bill knew that his situation was well beyond his ability to handle on his own and he knew from his years in the business world that leaving the insurance company to set the value of his claim on their own did not make sense. So, after meeting with us, he retained our firm to represent him on his claim.

Even though Bill had purchased a very good insurance policy from one of the largest insurance companies in America, it took the claims department 14 days before they even made their first visit to Bill's home. During this first meeting, representatives from the insurance company spent several hours writing up their damage evaluation for Bill's home on their laptop computer. At the end of this first meeting, they confirmed that they had completed their damage evaluation, but they told us that they were not authorized to share their evaluation until it was approved by management. It was another 36 days before we finally got a glimpse at their evaluation and we were extremely disappointed to find that the total was for less than half of the damages we had agreed to with them at their initial inspection.

We quickly proceeded to prepare a reconciliation to itemize the differences between their evaluation and ours and we set another meeting to resolve those differences. At that meeting, the insurance company representatives politely advised us that they would take our concerns under consideration, discuss them with their management, and get back to us. It was all too clear that the adjusters representing one of the largest insurance companies in the country had no authority to settle a claim and must instead ask for approval to pay the claim from supervisors who have never even seen the damages. It has now been 3 more weeks and we are still awaiting their reply.

Last week, we were informed that Bill was experiencing high anxiety and significant stress, which is likely the result of his unresolved claim situation. In fact, Bill even went to see his doctor over these issues.

People react to stressful situations in different ways, and medical science has shown there is a causative link between emotional stress and physical manifestations.

Today, we learned that Bill was admitted last night to the hospital following a severe stroke and was in the intensive care unit in serious condition. They performed surgery early this morning, but Bill's full recovery is a question. You might think ...*all this over an insurance claim?*...but what you must remember is that this is a lot more than just an insurance claim to Bill... this is his life and his life's accumulation of things that are all personal and important to him and his wife. The water loss was only the first tragedy. The bigger tragedy ended up being the insurance company's game- playing and the excessive delays that are deliberately designed to wear down the consumer and reduce the insurance companies' liability for damages.

At this point, it is unclear how Bill and Ruth's situation will turn out or how Bill will recover from the stroke. But what is clear is that the actions of Bill's insurance company are not by accident. This is just one example of the insurance industry's high stakes game of low- balling the customer for their own profit. This practice is far more common today than it was in years past. Insurance companies know that by offering low-ball claim settlements, and then delaying the process for as long as possible, they can get many claimants to simply give up and just take what they can get without a fight. Let's face it, most people who have had a loss do not want years of litigation in order to be paid fairly for their claim. They just want their lives put back together as quickly as possible. The insurance companies know this and they use this motivation against their customers, to reduce their claims payments. You see, every dollar saved on claims payments is another dollar of profit that drops directly to the insurance company's bottom line.

To the insurance industry, this is nothing more than a game; a *Claims Game*. To the homeowner or business owner who may have just lost everything they own to a fire, a windstorm, or some other tragedy, it certainly is no game to them. But the sad truth is to the insurance company, the consumer has become a pawn in a high stakes game of "catch us if you can" and "hide and go seek" your claims payments. It is just such real-life experiences that we have personally experienced with our clients over the last three decades that gave rise to the idea for the book, *The Claims Game*. As we have recently reassessed the current state of the claims business, it has become clear that the contractual promise that the insurance companies make with their insurance policy's promise of coverage for a loss is more often today a **Broken Promise**.

The problems with achieving fair claim settlements have become epidemic in America as insurance companies have become more blatant than ever before in their disrespect for their customers and more indifferent to fulfilling their contractual promises. And justice is not easily found, as some recent court rulings have gutted consumers' ability to hold insurance companies accountable for their wrongful conduct through bad faith punitive damage awards.

To help you better understand the rules that govern insurance, lets briefly explain the term "tort" and the concept of insurance "bad faith." A tort is a wrongful act, other than a breach of contract, which unfairly causes someone else to suffer loss or harm. The remedy for a tort in civil courts is a monetary award for the damages suffered. In Arizona, as in most other jurisdictions, the tort of bad faith arises when an insurer intentionally denies or fails to process or pay a claim without a reasonable basis. These courts recognize that an insurance policy (contract) is not an ordinary commercial bargain and that implicit in an insurance contract and in the insurance relationship is the insurer's promise to play fairly with its' insured. The Arizona courts described this duty in the *Rawlings*[1] case, where the Arizona Supreme court concluded that the insurer has "some duties of a fiduciary nature," including "equal consideration, fairness and honesty." The insurance company has an obligation to immediately conduct a reasonable investigation, act reasonably in evaluating the claim and act promptly in paying a legitimate claim. If an insurer acts unreasonably in the manner in which it processes a claim, it can be held liable for bad faith, which can result in punitive damages.

The idea of bad faith and punitive damages is a concept that was designed into our legal system to deter businesses and individuals from deliberately engaging in wrongful conduct. The idea is to award punitive damages to the wronged party to discourage a specific wrongdoer and other potential future wrongdoers, from knowingly and deliberately engaging in wrongful conduct in the future. An award of punitive damages is intended to place a monetary penalty on the wrongdoer to deter misconduct and make such misconduct too expensive to be a viable business practice. Sort of a legal version of, "hit them where it hurts most; in their wallets". For instance, if an insurance company deliberately engages in wrongful conduct as described above, and is later held liable to pay only the contract damages that they owed in the first place, where is the incentive for them to act properly?

One major factor that has set in motion the increase we are seeing in wrongful claims conduct was the United States Supreme Court's ruling in *Campbell v. State Farm*[2], wherein the court ruled that a $145 million-dollar punitive damages award that was upheld against State Farm by the Utah Supreme Court was excessive. The United States Supreme Court held that even in the most extreme circumstances, the multiplier for punitive damage awards should not exceed a "single digit" multiplier of the contract damages. What this means is that according to this ruling, a multiplier of 9X times the actual damages are as much as is reasonable under the law. The court's decision was based on the "due process" clause found in the fourteenth amendment of the Constitution. Many state courts have taken this decision and have narrowed the punitive damage award guidelines even further, some ruling that punitive damages should not exceed a ratio of one to one. What this means to a consumer is that the courts have given the insurance companies a license to steal from their customers. How do you deter a multi-billion dollar insurance company from committing egregious acts against their policyholders if the mechanism of justice has no teeth, no deterrent ability? In particular, if an insurance company cheats millions of people out of a small to moderate amount of money, this is highly profitable for the insurance company, but is very hard for the cheated consumer to make right.

The best defense consumers had before *Campbell* was that a deliberately deceptive insurance practice, even over a relatively small amount of money, could result in a huge punitive damage award. This concept is best illustrated by the Arizona court's ruling in *Hawkins v. Allstate*[3], where Allstate was caught wrongfully withholding $35.00 per claim for final cleaning on auto claims for total loss vehicles. The court

calculated the number of claims Allstate had processed in this manner over a certain period of time to determine the reasonable punishment. This pre-Campbell ruling ultimately cost Allstate $3.5 million in punitive damages. That's right, $3.5 million on a damage claim of $35.00. What better way to get an incredibly rich insurance company's attention than to expose them to substantial punitive damages for willful breaches of their duty to act in good faith.

Today, under *Campbell*, the most *Hawkins* would be able to recover would be $315.00 in punitive damages, or 9 times the contract damages amount. For a multi-billion dollar insurance company, this potential penalty limitation is certainly not much of a deterrent. So, the reality is that insurance companies have been emboldened and have become more difficult than ever to hold accountable for their wrongful conduct. And this lack of consequences has exacerbated the problems consumers face when they file an insurance claim.

Even more disturbing is that the smaller the amount of the dispute, the more unlikely that the customer will receive justice. For instance, let's assume that your claim was significant, say $100,000, but through a painstaking process of battling with your insurer, you have gotten the difference down to $20,000. What attorney is going to take on an insurance bad faith case for $20,000? While you may get lucky and find one, the chances are he will not be a top-tier attorney, because there is simply not enough potential recovery to make this fight worth the attorney's time. And a battle it will be, as insurance companies fight consumers even harder in litigation than they do during the claims process.

Recently, we have been working hail damage claims in northern Arizona. Of the 27 claims we have adjusted, eight of them under the nation's largest insurer and only this insurer had taken the wrongful position that there is no hail damage on these roofs. If I put these claims on an aerial view map and highlighted the ones that have been denied versus the paid claims. It is readily apparent that these claims truly should have hail damage as they are intermixed with all the other homes where their insurers paid their claims. Our clients cannot understand how their next-door neighbor got his roof damages paid, but his insurer is refusing to accept coverage for their loss. They, as expected, are totally frustrated with the position their insurer has taken, but with each of these claims being less than $20,000, justice will be very difficult and costly to achieve.

One might suggest demanding appraisal to resolve this dispute, but the insurers denial of coverage for this loss takes the appraisal resolution out of the equation, as coverage disputes are not subject to resolution by appraisal. These policyholders are left with little choice but to just leave the damages as they are or pay out of pocket for repairs.

Insurance companies fully realize they are unlikely to be held accountable for wrongdoing on these smaller claims, which essentially gives them a license to steal.

It is a travesty that consumers must hire claims professionals or attorneys to get what they paid for when they bought their insurance policies. Even more outrageous is the fact that consumers must fight and even litigate to hold their insurance company accountable and to assure that they are paid fairly and in accordance with the policy's promise of coverage. Much has been written on this subject, including a very insightful investigative report several years ago in Bloomberg Magazine called the *Insurance Hoax*[4]. Unfortunately, nothing has really changed since that article was written. In fact, the problem seems to have only gotten worse as insurers find that handling claims like they are has led to even great profits. This is the new reality of the insurance business today. It is important for consumers to be aware, not only of the game, but how it is played, as knowing and understanding the game can place the consumer on a more equal footing with their insurance company.

Chapter Two

"Trouble…Trouble, Trouble; A New Perspective"

What we often hear from potential clients is, "Why would I need my own adjuster, doesn't the insurance company provide me with an adjuster?" The answer to this question is both yes and no. Yes, they do provide an adjuster to investigate and settle your claim, but no, that adjuster does not truly represent your interests; instead, they are there to represent the insurance company's interests.

The business of insurance has undergone significant changes in America over the last 20 years. Gone are the days when an insurance company viewed their job as a true fiduciary responsibility of collecting premiums from a large group of people and paying out fairly to customers who experience a loss, thus fulfilling their promise to protect their customers in their time of need. Have you noticed how all the old commercials and slogans which used to run constantly on television and radio have all changed in their messaging? Gone are all the timeless slogans telling you how much you can depend upon your insurance company to protect you in the event of a loss and what great partners in the community they are; slogans like, "You're in Good Hands…"; "Like a Good Neighbor…; and, of course "…Fast, Fair & Friendly."

Today, their commercials are designed to send a different message. They now intentionally downplay how much of a partner they will be during a time of loss, and instead have adopted more generic themes. Themes such as, losses can happen, you need to insure yourself from them. Ads like Allstate's "Mayhem" commercials where Mayhem is causing all sorts of destruction. And Liberty Mutual's "humans… imperfect people living in an imperfect world… responsibility, what's your policy," According to Consumer Reports[5] ratings, Allstate and Liberty Mutual are both near the bottom of their list of good insurance companies. It has been our experience that you may not truly understand what mayhem is until you file a claim with Allstate. And from our dealings with Liberty Mutual, it is clear that if responsibility was actually was their policy we would be out of a job.

There are also those cute new Farmer's University commercials, but it is still unclear as to how the stupid looks on those student adjusters' faces might inspire someone to want them adjusting their next insurance claim. More recently, Farmers has started advertising various extreme situation in ads like the moose caught in the swing set where are say "we covered that!" So, if a moose gets caught up in your kid's swing set, they will cover the damages, but God forbid you have a fire loss or hail damage to your home, you might see completely different treatment and you might see a whole bunch of damages that they "Don't Cover." And, of course, our favorite because we are dog lovers, the Traveler's dog with the bone and the music playing the words in the background "trouble…trouble, trouble,…" as he dreams about losing his bone. The poor dog doesn't realize that, based on our experience the insurance company he insured his bone with is the one most likely to actually steal it!

The changes in the way they market their products are not by accident. They are a clear indication of how they have changed their view of their relationship with their customers. They no longer care if you are unhappy with their claims settlements or that you might decide to change insurance companies. There are millions of other customers out there that are equally unhappy with their current insurance companies who will be knocking on their door for a new insurance policy. The business of insurance is no longer about providing a good product, good service and customer retention; it is purely and simply about reducing claims costs and increasing net profits.

We constantly talk with people who are under the delusion that their insurance company actually values their business. We often hear comments of shock like this one from a recent client: *"I have been a customer of XYZ Insurance for 28 years and I have never had a claim until now; and then they just drop me over this one claim."* Most people find it hard to believe how quickly they can go from being a valued customer (a loss free premium paying policyholder) to a liability (a customer with a claim to be paid).

The modern view of insurance companies is on profits…profits… profits and more profits. This is what drives their management and the enormous bonuses they can receive for holding claims costs down and it is what satisfies their shareholders. How did this transformation happen? How did we get here?

Many industry experts[6] agree that these changes have a direct correlation with the separation of Allstate Insurance Company from their parent company Sears & Roebuck in the early 1990's. For those of you not from that generation, up until the early 1990's, Allstate was a part of Sears & Roebuck. In the 60's and 70's we could go down to the local Sears & Roebuck store with Dad to buy a new hammer, pick up a couple dress shirts for Dad and pay our car insurance bill to the handy agent who for years usually sat at an Allstate booth near the escalator.

Around 1992, the Allstate Insurance Company engaged the services of international business consulting firm McKinsey & Company with the idea of remaking the company from the top down to make it more profitable. You may recall McKinsey was associated with the collapsed Enron Corporation, which was called the house that McKinsey built[7].

For more than a year, McKinsey's legions of MBA's worked in every department analyzing Allstate's business operations. They looked analytically at every process as a function that can either generate more revenues or as an expense that can be better managed. McKinsey made their recommendations to Allstate via several PowerPoint[8] slide presentations in 1992, but, it wasn't until 2001 that the contents of these presentations became public, and only via a direct court order and after a monumental effort by Allstate's attorneys to keep its' contents secret.

McKinsey's advice

"SIT AND WAIT"
McKinsey told Allstate it could wear down customers by delaying settlements and stalling court proceedings.

"ZERO-SUM ECONOMIC GAME"
The consulting firm said there are winners and losers. Allstate can win by paying out no more than it has to, so it can keep more of its premium income.

"GOOD HANDS OR BOXING GLOVES"
McKinsey suggested Allstate politely make a low offer on a claim. If a policyholder protests or hires a lawyer, the insurer should fight back.

Source: A videotape of a hearing in Fayette Circuit Court in Lexington, Kentucky.

What McKinsey recommended was a complete transformation of the "philosophy" of Allstate's business model from the traditional customer service focus to a profit-centric focus. McKinsey easily identified that the largest expense on the insurance company's profit & loss statement was for claims expenses (i.e. claims payments). So the natural solution to increasing Allstate's profits was quite simply; reduce claims payments.

In order to better understand this monumental transformation of the business of insurance, it is important that you understand some of the basic tenets of insurance. The first is the indemnity principle which is the overall purpose of property insurance. These policies promise to indemnify the policyholder or restore them to the same financial position after the loss as they were before the loss. To indemnify someone is to make them whole. So under a fire insurance policy, the insurance company promises to make the policyholder whole, up to the limits of the policy, in exchange for the policyholder's payment in the form of a policy premium.

Another important concept is that of the fiduciary principle which has been the basic tenant of insurance law for nearly a century. The fiduciary principle was designed to balance the relationship between the insurance company and their policyholder. Under this principle, the insurance companies' act much like a bank, holding the insureds' money (premiums) and of course investing it until these funds are needed to pay out on a claim. It is a sacred trust placed with these insurance companies thereby they hold all of these policyholders' premiums in an account and then pay out fairly to restore those insureds that have suffered a covered loss.

The changes recommended by McKinsey & Company and implemented then by Allstate completely transformed the business of insurance, not just for Allstate, but it would ultimately change the entire insurance industry. The changes implemented transformed the insurance industry from the traditional business model of collecting premiums from a large group of customers and then paying the fair value for claims to those who incur a loss (a fiduciary responsibility) to a profit-focused model that ignored the fair indemnification of the policyholder to restore him to his pre-loss financial condition. Likewise, it simultaneously ignored other business principles like customer satisfaction and customer retention in favor of profits. Under this new philosophy the expense of claims payments was now fair game to manage "for profit" and the cost of claims was now viewed as a profit center to pad their bottom line.

To better understand the changes that were being recommended, we need look no further than some of McKinsey's PowerPoint slides that were used in their presentation to the executives of Allstate. The most telling of these slides suggested that the business of insurance is a "Zero Sum Game." This means that in order for someone to win, someone must lose. To put this idea into better perspective, let's rephrase this as it was to be applied at Allstate: "If Allstate is to win, their customers must lose." It is an interesting business philosophy. How many policies do you think they would sell using this as their advertising slogan? Imagine if they changed their slogan from; "You're in good hands with Allstate" to "If Allstate is going to make a huge profit, our customers must lose."

It seems that McKinsey's team of MBA's must have taken the lessons from the 1987 movie Wall Street to heart. You may recall Michael Douglas' character's infamous line, "Greed is good!" This was the revolutionary new business philosophy that was being proposed to Allstate.

Other slides suggested that Allstate offer a quick low-ball claim settlement and if the customer did not take it, then it was time to "Put down the Good Hands and Pick up the Boxing Gloves."[9] Another slide focused on other opportunities for Allstate to improve profits by working to keep their policyholders from retaining professional representation, stating "Even greater opportunity exists to prevent claimants from becoming represented (Payments on represented claims is on average five times the size of unrepresented claims)." In other words, keep our policyholders from hiring representation, because it will cost us more money.

And, of course, the most famous of their slides gave this new philosophy for doing business a moniker. They called it the "Three D's" which stood for Delay, Deny and Defend. In other words, delay the claim as long as possible, deny claims as often as they can and then defend these denials to the end. Make the process so difficult that consumers just give up rather than fight.

In his book *From Good Hands To Boxing Gloves*[10], *attorney and author* David Berardinelli brilliantly illustrates to the reader how the changes implemented by Allstate fly in the face of proper insurance conduct. He compares buying of a can of peas to buying an insurance policy. In his example, he suggests that what if you go to the store and buy a 10-ounce can of peas, but when you get home and open the can, you find it only has 7 ounces of peas in the can. So you take the can of peas back to the store and complain and they give you another can of peas. However, when you get home and open the can you find that it too has only 7 ounces of peas in it. Of course, your first thought would be that this must be some kind of mistake. Maybe the machine needs to be recalibrated. But, what if you found out that the pea company had deliberately set their machine to only fill the 10 ounce can with 7 ounces of peas so as to produce windfall profits for the pea company's shareholders and huge bonuses for their executives? Most people would call this fraud.

Allstate Insurance Company's implementation of this new claims handling philosophy had dramatic effects on their company's operating income. In the ten-year period before implementation of the McKinsey program, Allstate's average annual pre-tax operating income was approximately $82 million per year. In the eleven-year period after implementation of the McKinsey program, Allstate's average pre-tax operating income grew to $2.5 billion annually, an incredible 3,335% increase. It did not take long for other insurance companies and their stockholders to take notice and begin the implementation of similar changes to duplicate these sorts of profit results for themselves and their shareholders. And, McKinsey was not the only one making these types of bold recommendations. About this same time another major consulting firm, Accenture[11], was giving similar advice to their insurance company clients.

This new focus on claims expenses as a profit center has completely changed the relationship between the insurance company and the consumer. Now, in order to get fair treatment on the settlement of claims, it is unlikely to be achieved without the services of a claims professional, i.e. a public adjuster or an attorney.

People are resistant to change by nature and insurance company employees are no exception. To curb internal resistance from the claims departments, the insurance companies have little by little, pushed out those seasoned company adjusters who resisted these new claim procedures. Many of these seasoned adjusters knew that they were being asked to handle claims in a manner that was contrary to the practices and procedures that had learned through their years of insurance training. Those who were willing to stay were forced to accept the new claims handling procedures or were replaced with new inexperienced and poorly or intentionally mis-trained adjusters. The old industry adage is that the more educated the adjuster, the more he will pay on claims. The reason for this is that a competent professional knows what truly should be paid under the policy.

In our interactions with many of these older and more seasoned professional adjusters, it was made quite clear that they were not happy with the way their claims handling practices were being changed. Most were reluctant to process claims in the manner they are now being asked to, so many of them have either retired or may have sucked up their pride, turned a blind eye to these practices and are simply counting the days until retirement.

Then of course there are those that stayed who have bought into the new claim philosophy. This group of adjusters is the worst of the worst, as they are active participants in the abusive tactics being employed in the settlement of claims. These "company men" are willing to do whatever it takes to gain favor with management.

And these newly hired adjusters do not know any better than what they have been taught by the company on claims handling in their two-to-four-week training programs. There is no way in the time currently being allotted to properly train an adjuster to investigate claims, determine coverage, and estimate the value of loss. They rely upon their managers who tell them that "our policy does not cover this or that." They are being deliberately sent out to settle claims with little knowledge or even worse, misinformation. We often have encounters with adjusters who spew the company line, tell us that "our policy does not owe to match." Yet, when we hand them a copy of the policy and tell them to point out the language in the policy that says you do not owe to match, they routinely refuse to even look at the policy. Most often they tell us that it is in the policy and they are not obligated to show us where this provision is.

These "new age" claims adjusters are being assisted by insurance restoration contractors who routinely assist in preparing significantly deficient loss evaluations to gain favor with the insurance company. They are also being directed by management to work with approved experts/consultants who routinely report that there is no damage, or the damage is from another cause of loss not covered in the policy.

This new breed adjuster handles claims under a different playbook than in the past. Gone are the days when an adjuster had reasonable settlement authority to resolve claims up to his authority limit. In the old days, as adjusters became more experienced in claims handling, their settlement authority was increased by management, giving them the ability to use their superior training and skills to settle claims fairly and in accordance with the terms of the policy.

Today, few insurers that give adequate settlement authority to their adjusters and many now that give virtually no authority at all. We are constantly engaged with senior large loss adjusters who only have very little in settlement authority and must go through this same process of approval to get claim payments issued.

Most insurers have gone to a claim manager or claim committee review system where the field adjuster has no authority whatsoever to issue claim payments. Today's adjuster prepares his report and makes his recommendation for settlement of the claim to a claims manager or claims committee, who review his report and either approves or request revisions. We assume that when they request a revision, it is not to pay the customer more money. And you might ask how is a claims manager or a committee in a better position to determine the fair value of a claims that they have never seen?

This process makes the job of settling a claim far more time consuming and difficult because we typically wait weeks for a management response and all claim negotiations must be communicated through the adjuster who is just a messenger boy in this process. Not only must you convince the adjuster of the proper payment of damages, but you must train him on how to convince his manager or claim committee of their necessity. To give you a clearer understanding of how these changes can lead to excessive delays in claim payments, the following quotation is from an email we recently received on a claim that has been in processing by one of the 3 largest insurers in the nation for more than a year and a half: *"My timeline from last week was delayed as the payment has been sent up from my supervisor, to the manager, to the territory manager, then to the regional manager. They have a meeting to approve tomorrow, as I have been routinely asking for status checks on the approval."*

The process for approving claim payments has been deliberately modified to cause an intentional delay the payment of claims. Instead of having a competent adjuster who has authority to issue claim payments, the adjusters today must go to their supervisor, to a manager to a territory manager and then to a regional manager before a payment can be issued for $30,000. Adjusting claims in this manner give the insurer a great deal of time to scrutinize the loss evaluation and think of ways to deny legitimate construction line items in the loss evaluation.

We believe that handling claims in this manner is a violation of the promise of the policy, which says the insurance company will negotiate the claim with you, the consumer or your representative. If you or your representative never get an audience (meeting) with someone from the insurance company who actually has authority to negotiate the settlement of your claim, how does this claim payment system fulfill their promise? Most policies contain language that generally states; "We (the insurance company) will adjust the loss with You (the insured)..." but, how can they fulfill this promise, if you never get to see the man behind the curtain or actually engage in negotiations with him?

Over the last fifteen years, these new procedures for claims handling seem to have gone on steroids, as we are seeing an ever-increasing trend of wrongful denials of coverage; significant underpayment of claims (low-balling); deliberate omissions of damages and an array of other improper claims handling practices. This new process has also spawned a drastic increase in the numbers of insurance experts/consultants, who are more than happy to do the insurance industry's bidding for them. Insurance companies are now constantly in need of expert reports that say there is no damage to the insured's property or that say the damages are related to something other than that which is covered by the insurance policy.

It is estimated that fewer than 5% of all claimants retain professional representation to settle their claims. If you are one of the many who is trying to deal with the aftermath of a major property damage claim, it is our hope and purpose in this book to arm you with information that will help you to identify some of the tricks and deceptions that are most commonly used by the insurance companies today to intentionally underpay your claim.

More importantly, we hope to make you aware of the importance of claim representation in receiving fair treatment from your insurer. A competent professional adjuster can help navigate the highly complex problems with adjusting a claim and recovering the full fair value of loss. The reality is that insurance companies do not pay adjusters bonuses for paying more on claims.

Chapter Three

Rules of the Game

In order to compete and win in the insurance industry's high stakes **Claims Game**, you must first understand the game and how it is played by the insurance companies. Like the game of chess, you cannot win if you do not know how the pieces move. As noted in the previously released book the **Claims Game**, the moves are not just about strategy, but they start with understanding what everyone's interest is in your claim proceeds are. Once you understand all the varied interests, you can begin to make informed decisions to protect your own interests, instead of relying upon other people to tell you what to do. This will help you to develop a winning strategy for your claim recovery.

The insurance company's first move is most often to send out a very charming claims adjuster to set your mind at ease that they are there to help you through this tragic event. He sometimes comes with a check book in hand; ready to write you a relatively insignificant check to help you through the next few days. He will often times warn you about all the predatory Public Adjusters who will try to sign you to a contract. This warning is often echoed by insurance agents and many of the insurance industry's restoration contractors. They will explain that public adjusters cannot get you any more than the Insurance

Company is going to pay you anyway without their help, so by engaging them you are just giving way some of your money. So, as a public service and out of the goodness of their hearts, they will tell you to avoid these Public Adjuster people. Are you overwhelmed by their concern yet?

The reality is often far different. Like any industry there are both good and bad representatives, and public adjusting is no exception. Whether or not you decide to retain a public adjuster should be your decision alone and it should not be made without careful consideration. The larger point here is that it is not your money that the insurance company is truly concerned with. They are concerned that, as you will recall from the previous chapter, "represented claims payout five times more than unrepresented claims." Consequentially, the insurance company has a serious financial interest in discouraging claimants from hiring representation. Remember that in the insurance company's profit and loss statement, claim payments is the largest expense item. For every dollar saved in claims payments, that dollar flows through the financial report to the bottom line; i.e., the net profit.

Next, you might question why your agent, whom you have known for years, might care if you retain representation. After all, he is supposed to be on your side in this matter. The truth is, that many agents have their own incentive to keep you from hiring representation. Most agents are paid based upon a formula that takes the total of the premiums collected on the insurance policies they sell and then subtracts the amounts of claims paid out on those policies before they calculate their sales commissions and/or annual bonus. The insurance company's goal is to reward the writing of good (claims free) business.

A few years ago in a litigated claim, we had an agent who was questioned under oath as to why the insurance company's claim file showed that he had called both the adjuster and the claims manager multiple times to object to their intended payment of this huge fire loss claim. He refused to accept the adjuster's determination that the claim was legitimate and went over his head to his supervisor and eventually was successful in getting the insurance company to deny coverage for the loss. After hours of excruciating questioning, he eventually admitted that when the company eventually was forced by the evidence to pay this claim it wiped out his substantial five figure year-end agency bonus.

Therefore, your agent may or may not really be concerned with your interests as much as his own. This is certainly not an indictment of all agents. Most are good people who are truly interested in their customers getting fair treatment. Many I am sure would be happy to forgo their bonus in order for their customers to be treated fairly. Unfortunately, human nature cannot be blindly dismissed either. There are some who will place their own financial interests above their customer's interests. Which agent you have is something you will need to decide for yourself. Our purpose here is to simply explain the varying interests when a claim is filed so that you can make a better informed decision.

Why would a restoration contractor care if you hire a public adjuster? Most restoration contractors get the majority of their business from insurance companies and many public adjusters have their own preferred contractors. Insurance restoration contractors rely heavily upon insurance companies to make their living. If they can encourage consumers to not hire a public adjuster, they stand a much better chance of getting the job themselves and, at the very least, they are making brownie points with the assigned adjuster, who will likely respond favorably with other work for them.

More importantly, if you do retain the insurance companies preferred contractor, there is a reasonable chance that this contractor is more interested in the insurance companies' interests than in yours, their customer. Just as with agents and company adjusters, the restoration contractor likewise has a financial incentive to favor the insurance company, as they get much of their work from them. If a dispute arises over whether or not the interior walls can be saved, whose side do you think the contractor is really on? Hopefully it is on yours.

Another financial interest in your insurance claim proceeds is that of the adjuster who is assigned to settle your claim. While it is considered improper within the insurance industry for an insurance company to provide financial incentives to their adjusters which might encourage them to underpay claims, the fact is adjuster bonuses are still commonplace and they can significantly impact your claim settlement.

Having been involved in many dozens of insurance bad faith litigations, we find that most insurance companies have some sort of performance bonus program to incentivize their adjusters to meet the company's objectives. Over the years, this practice has been the source of many litigations where the courts have ruled this practice to be a violation of the insurance company's duty of good faith under the insurance policy. Due to these costly bad faith rulings, these programs have become more discreet in their true purpose by including other metrics such as good customer service, good claims handling practices, the speed that the claim is closed, and other measures of their performance. But make no mistake about it, nearly all of these programs contain some element that is tied to the financial performance of the insurance company and, in reality we believe that this is actually their true measure of performance. While we have had most adjuster's, even under oath, emphatically deny that they get any incentives for the company's financial performance, once we question them further and get into the details of their bonus programs, it is clear that most have hidden incentives built into their bonus programs.

Insurance companies are constantly focused on controlling costs. Adjusters can save very little money on office supplies, but significant underpayments of claims can drastically improve the insurance company's bottom line.

In the insurance business, the most important measure of profitability is known as the "combined ratio" which is the claims expenses, plus the other cost of claims, divided by the total premiums collected. This ratio helps insurance companies to measure their performance. Nearly every adjuster bonus program we have seen, no matter how well it is disguised, includes the metric of meeting the company's combined ratio objectives. You might wonder how this is important to you.

When you have a claim, the cost of your claim to the insurance company gets added into the combined ratio along with all the other claims and claim expenses. The less money the adjuster pays you, the better the company's combined ratio becomes. If claim adjusters are incentivized to reduce claim payments to secure substantial bonuses, this creates a significant conflict of interest and it can affect their ability to be objective in their loss determinations.

In the insurance litigation business, we refer to these types of adjuster incentive programs as "institutional bad faith" programs. It is considered bad faith for an insurance company to create a program that encourages their adjusters or provides an incentive for them to underpay a legitimate claim. Most insurance companies have taken drastic steps to hide or mask these programs in response to large bad faith damages awards, but the fact is, many still have some bonus programs that considers the company's meeting of their combined ratio or financial goals.

Another interest in your claim proceeds is that of the emergency services restoration company. These are the people that your agent or the person at the insurance company's claims hotline refer you to immediately to assist in the cleanup and security of the property until they get an adjuster assigned to your claim. This is the first step in the claims process to put you on the road to recovery. These alleged "experts" will come into your home or business to give you advice on what must be done to protect the property from further damage. This advice is important, because under the policies' terms and conditions is the requirement that you (the insured) take all reasonable steps to protect the property from further damage.

These emergency restoration contractors come referred by your insurance company and you are encouraged to hire them to complete necessary emergency services.

And make no mistake about it; you may have hired this contractor to work for you, but his real customer is the insurance company. This is the old chicken or the egg analogy. In this relationship, you are the egg, the insurance company is the chicken; and the chicken keeps laying these eggs. So, whose interests do you think is the most important to this contractor? He was brought there and/or referred by the insurance company for a reason. It is because he has shown himself to be a willing partner in helping the insurance company reduce their claim costs. If a dispute arises over whether or not a sofa can be cleaned, he will nearly always take the insurance adjusters position, unless he and the adjuster are working to gain your confidence in him, then they may sacrifice an item or two, to show how he is really working for you, but be aware and be skeptical.

While these services are often necessary to prevent further damages, what you must realize is that by signing their "blank work authorization" form, you have just given this contractor a blank check to spend your money. Worst yet is that most of these work authorization forms include a direct payment authorization, meaning that you have told your insurance company that they can pay these people directly out of your (money) claim proceeds.

Most people do not realize that it is not the insurance company's money at that point; it is their claim money that is being spent on these services. By signing a direct payment authorization, you have just relinquished total control over your claim to this contractor. What often happens is that the emergency services work turns into additional work, such as packing up all of the home's contents and removing it for storage and safe keeping while the structure damages are repaired.

By turning over control of the money, you have no recourse should their work not be satisfactory. We recently had a relative who signed a direct pay authorization after a serious water loss. After all of his personal property was returned, he found deep gouges in some of his furniture, a torn mattress cover and many missing items. Because of the direct payment authorization he signed, this contractor was paid in full for their work, so it was a nightmare to negotiate a fair settlement of the damages and then it was another three months wait to get their refund check.

While many of these restoration services can be truly necessary, we often see restoration contractors spending tens of thousands of dollars of customer's claim money to inventory their property, wrap and pack it into boxes, move it to a climate-controlled storage facility and store this property, which on day-one should have been identified as non- salvageable items. In layman's terms, this means that the property was a total loss and spending large sums of your money to pack it up in bubble wrap, move it to a climate-controlled storage warehouse and paying exurbanite charges to store this property is a huge waste of your claim money. It is not uncommon for a pack-out/in on a residential claim to exceed $30,000 and on a commercial claim it can be significantly more.

This really becomes a problem when your damages exceed your policy limits of coverage. It is not until then that consumers find that this wasted money could have been used to replace damaged property rather than be wasted at the insurance company's encouragement. Of course, the insurance company takes no responsibility for this waste of your money because they were your contractor, not theirs. Remember that blank work authorization form you signed?

Moreover, we often find restoration contractors attempting to restore items that truly cannot be restored, and they get encouragement from the company adjuster, because cleaning items is much cheaper than replacing them and from the restoration company's perspective they do not get paid for items that are not cleaned because they are a total loss. So there is an incentive by both the insurance company and the restoration company to attempt to clean everything, even truly uncleanable items.

Make no mistake about it, no matter how large or nationally known the restoration contractor is, they have a financial incentive to support the insurance companies' interests. It is a matter of survival.

Just recently, we represented a couple who's water supply line to the toilet upstairs broke while they were out of town. When they got home, they found that the ceiling in their kitchen and family room had collapsed and the house was full of water. When we arrived, the national emergency services contractor was already on scene doing the water extraction. After our inspection with an infrared camera to determine which areas had hidden water damage within their walls, we explained that we wanted all of these wet areas drywall removed.

This started an argument with the restoration contractor who insisted that these walls did not need to be removed and even suggested that wet drywall is actually stronger than new drywall because when it is dried out, it becomes harder. Even knowing our firms' credentials, he insisted upon getting the insurance company's adjusters approval before he would remove these walls. Certainly, there can be no question as to who this national restoration contractor perceives to be their customer and it surely was not the homeowner.

We recently represented a church who was encouraged by their insurance adjuster to hire a national restoration company to clean a huge portion of their classroom building for smoke damage following the fire. This was done months before they hired us. By the time we were retained, this restoration contractor had racked up an incredible $870,000 in cleaning costs, bringing in workers from out of state and adding their hotel rooms to their bill, along with massive amounts of overtime. But, to add insult to injury, the portion of the building that they cleaned has now been required by the City's Building Department to be completely torn down. This adjuster never investigated the status of this building with the City before recommending the expenditure of hundreds of thousands of dollars to clean a building that ultimately must be demolished. And he never told the church that they did not have to engage this company in order to recover the money for the cleaning. The church surely could have put this money to better use if they had been given the proper advice, but both the insurance company adjuster and the restoration contractor were too busy worrying about their own interests to worry about the customers.

Also, be careful about relying upon restoration companies to take a physical inventory of your property. It is not their money and many of the people these restoration companies hire are minimum wage, daily labor workers who could care less about the accuracy of their listing. It takes a great deal of time and effort to prepare a proper and complete personal property inventory. Over the years, we have found entire rooms that were accidentally left off these restoration contractor inventories and have reviewed inventories that did not provide adequate details and descriptions to competently evaluate the current replacement cost of the destroyed items.

If the item is not correctly described, it cannot be correctly priced for its' current replacement cost price. For instance, we recently handled a water loss claim in Texas where the master bedroom inventory included 18 pairs of men's dress shoes that the insurance company priced at $100.00 per pair. After interviewing the insured, we discovered that most of these shoes were from Bruno Magli, Magnolini, and Mezlan with a couple pairs of Louis Vuitton shoes thrown in. These are all very expensive imported men's shoes with average values above $500.00 per pair or more. This is an example of how easily a bad item description can affect the value of the claim.

Now that we have covered the varying interests in your claim recovery by the insurance company, their adjuster, your agent, the restoration contractor and the emergency services restoration contractors, let's turn our attention to the claim process itself. After the insurance company has their emergency restoration contractor busy extracting water and cleaning everything in sight, their next move is to develop a building loss evaluation that is allegedly intended to restore your home or building to its' pre-loss condition. Unfortunately, more often than not, their initial loss evaluations only account for a fraction of the actual costs required to restore your property. They offer you this quick low-ball settlement check and hope that you will go away. It is our experience that the initial claim settlement offers on average about 1/3 of the true value of loss. How can an insurance company's loss evaluations be so for off? It is by design!

This is how the program that was created by the business consultants at McKinsey is designed to work. They offer you a quick low-ball claim settlement and if you object to the amount, they put you through hell to get the balance of your rightful indemnity. In other words, they put down the "Good Hands and pick up Boxing Gloves." They deliberately cause excessive delays in your claim's handling. Those who object to the company's claim payment are placed on the back burner and left to simmer for an extended period of time. Fighting a multi-billion-dollar insurance company can be a daunting task, especially if you do not have the training and skills needed to win this negotiation. During a recent litigation, we ran across a page from a major insurance company's training manual whereby they were teaching their adjusters to negotiate claims by using the "Power of the Checkbook." What they were saying was that the insurance company has the money in their bank account and the customer who just had a loss needs this money to recover. So, they instruct their adjusters to use their superior financial position to force a reduced settlement.

We use the word "negotiation" because that is essentially what an insurance claim is; a claim settlement is a negotiated settlement of estimated costs of repair. Most consumers have the misconception that a claim settlement is a finite number that can be calculated with exacting precision. They mistakenly believe that the insurance company's adjuster just needs to enter a few things into some computer program and out comes the claim value. The fact is a claim settlement is truly a negotiated estimate of the cost of repairs. If we were to have ten contractors or adjusters prepare their loss evaluation on the same claim, we will end up with ten different claim values.

How then does one determine what the correct value of a claim is? It comes down to understanding construction methods, looking critically at the operations that must be included in the loss evaluation and confirming the prices for each of these operations. It also often requires making a judgment call on what reasonably is necessary to restore the property to its' pre-loss condition. This is a highly technical process and one that takes years to learn. In fact, even most contractors that do not do insurance restoration work do not understand how to use the computer software that is required by the insurance industry for claim evaluations. A winning negotiation is the product of extensive construction experience, a vast knowledge of the estimating software and an understanding of the coverages provided in the insurance policy. You have heard the saying "knowledge is power," this could not be any truer than in the context of claim settlements.

Similarly, the negotiation of the claim settlement of personal or business property damages also requires training and expertise. Understanding cleaning techniques and understanding how smoke, heat and water travel through a building during a fire and knowing how heat smoke and water can affect various types of finishes and materials takes years to learn. Understanding which items respond well to cleaning and which ones have little chance of being restorable is also important. We often use a negotiating technique with insurance adjusters who are adamant that an item can be successfully cleaned. We tell them that we will allow them to test clean the item in dispute and if it does not clean to our satisfaction, they must pay the cost of cleaning from their claim investigation budget and not from the policyholder's insurance proceeds. If there truly is a question on the cleanability of an item, we let the facts speak for themselves. Most often they chose not to engage us in this claim "dance" and just agree to pay for the item.

These same issues also arise when working with dry-cleaning companies. They only get paid for cleaning items, so if they don't clean it they don't get paid. This creates an incentive to attempt to clean items that there is no chance of salvaging. Insurance company adjusters are more than willing partners to the drycleaners because paying $2.50 to clean a shirt is much cheaper than paying $45.00 to replace it. Don't be fooled by appearance! Many items can suffer hidden damage which may not be visible to the naked eye; i.e. electronic appliances may be harmed by the caustic acidity of soot and smoke that continues to damage electronic circuitry even after the item is allegedly cleaned and appears to be working fine. Fabrics (clothes-furniture-draperies) are subject to material deterioration from temperatures as low as 200 degrees. Even a small fire can quickly reach temperatures of 1700 degrees so beware of these conditions. Mold, mildew and other spore growths can occur inside walls and ceilings, which may result in health concerns for the occupants and can cause long-term additional damage to the structure.

The process of resolving your building or your contents damages can go one of two ways. Either your adjuster is willing to compromise to the point of resolving your claim or he will not. It is not uncommon for the adjuster to throw you a bone, meaning that if he underpays the claim by thousands of dollars he has tremendous latitude to offer some compromise amount to settle your claim. We recently had a commercial client that had repeatedly complained to the insurance company about the inadequacy of their settlement offer. By the time he was referred to us, he had had four different adjusters come out, each one giving him just a little bit more than the last. After our intervention, he recovered more than double the last adjuster's loss evaluation.

Most consumers go into the claims process ignorant of how this process really works and believing that insurance companies operate like other normal businesses. They blindly believe that insurance companies are honest business partners who make a promise, collect a policy premium and in the event of a loss, they determine the fair value of the claim and issue a check. The reality is that insurance companies have rigged the system so that their initial loss valuations are all substantially lower than the actual fair values of their consumer's claims. By low-balling every claim and making their customers fight for every dollar, they have dramatically increased their profit margins.

It is not uncommon after a loss for you to place an undue amount of trust in your insurance company. When your home or your business has just been destroyed, it is quite natural to feel vulnerable and hopeful that your insurer will do as they have promised. Most people find it hard to believe that a program like the one described here could exist in America. It truly is brilliantly shameful that the insurance industry has taken this approach to the settlement of claims, but this is in fact the new reality. These practices are here to stay, because there is just too much money at stake and these additional profits to an insurance company are like crack to a drug addict.

Most insurance companies have moved to claims management systems that take most of the discretion away from the field adjuster and places it in the hands of the claim manager or in some cases a committee of claims managers. This program is designed to control claims costs and it makes the process of negotiating a fair settlement much more difficult and vastly more time consuming. And time is not on the consumer's side. Remember, it is not the adjuster or his manager that are living in a hotel or in some temporary rental. It is not their business that has been interrupted and cannot fulfill their customer's orders. They get to go back to their homes every night after work without consequence. You, on the other hand, are the one who is inconvenienced, uncomfortable and day-by-day you become more motivated to settle your claim. They know this and they now have you just where they want you.

Remember the three "D's" Delay, Deny and Defend! Welcome to the delay stage. But, do not despair. It is not impossible to obtain a fair claim settlement in a reasonable amount of time with tenacity and a knowledge of the game you are playing. A winning negotiation starts with a highly trained expert negotiator, i.e. a public adjuster adjusters are properly trained, educated, and experienced. Ask for a resume of experience before hiring any public adjuster and double check their claims. Don't rely on a few reference letters from their past customers, as my people settle claims thinking they were paid fairly and never knowing that they were not.

If you are not up to the task of settling your claim yourself, then find people whom you can really count on to support your claim. Your negotiated settlement will only be as good as is your negotiator, so choose wisely.

Chapter Four

Rules of Appraisal and other Alternative Resolution Methods

What happens when the two sides to the policy cannot reach a settlement agreement on the claim? This is where the policy's appraisal clause comes in. Nearly all policies in America contain an appraisal clause, which is a mechanism for resolving a claim that is intended to be faster and less costly than litigation. An appraisal clause is simply an alternative dispute resolution method to resolve claims. If either you or the insurance company makes a demand for appraisal, participation in the process is mandatory in most cases and under certain circumstances. Due to the extensive list of scenarios where submission to appraisal might be avoided, we will suggest that you seek the advice of an attorney for advice on your specific situation. What is most important to remember is that the appraisal clause was written by insurance companies, for insurance companies, so the odds of getting a truly fair settlement in this process are somewhat stacked against you.

One of the reasons for this is because insurance companies work daily on tens of thousands of claims and they control billions of dollars, so there are no shortages of appraisers willing to represent their interests. For the consumer, the list is much shorter and truly qualified appraisers can be very difficult to find. It is possible; however, with a reasonable amount of effort and critical verification of their qualifications to find a competent consumer appraiser.

Once you are satisfied that you have found a competent and experienced insurance appraiser, the first task in the appraisal process is for your appraiser and their appraiser to provide each other with disclosure statements[12] setting forth their past and current relationships with their respective nominators. Generally, the appraisal provision only requires that the appraisers be competent and disinterested. This means someone of reasonable intelligence, not necessarily an expert in the issues of dispute and disinterested mean that they have no financial interest in the outcome of the appraisal. With only a few exceptions, an appraiser cannot work on a contingency fee agreement, as this would make him interested in the outcome.

The next step is for the appraisers to reach an agreement on a third person to serve as the Umpire. If they cannot agree upon an Umpire, they must submit a request to the nearest court having jurisdiction to have a judge appoint an Umpire. The Umpire is essentially the tie breaker in the appraisal process. The Umpire is nothing more than a third appraiser and he actually is limited in his authority, as he only decides on items that the other two appraisers cannot agree upon. In practice; however, Umpires often exercise a great deal more authority over the appraisal process than was intended, as these people are usually retired judges or mediators/arbitrators who are used to being in control of some dispute resolution process. Add to this the appraisers' fear of angering the Umpire which might lead them to rule against their nominator and you have an alternative dispute resolution system that does not always function as it was intended.

Next the two appraisers are instructed to conduct their inspections independent of each other and exchange their loss evaluations.

They are then to meet in an attempt to reach agreement on as much of the loss as possible and then those items that are still in dispute, are to be submitted to the Umpire for a ruling. The intent of appraisal is that the Umpire will decide upon one of the two the positions placed before him of the appraisers.

The appraisal award is final and binding upon both the consumer and the insurance company. Except under extremely rare circumstances involving fraud, collusion or mistake, the courts will not generally overturn an appraisal award.

A host of problems have arisen with the manipulation of this dispute resolution method. First and foremost is the problem with finding a good Umpire who does not favor insurance companies. The insurance industry controls a tremendous amount of money and power and by its nature requires huge staffs of attorneys, both in-house counsel and outside counsel. The sheer amount of legal work generated by insurance companies draws in many new lawyers looking for their first job out of law school. This creates significant numbers of attorneys who at least have somewhat of a defense background. Judges often come from the private sector law firms, consequentially, a disproportionate number of judges and mediators also seem to have an insurance defense background.

It has been our experience over the years and over the many hundreds of appraisals that our firm has been involved in that the Umpire candidates available tend to have disproportionate number with backgrounds in insurance defense work. This does not necessarily mean to say that these candidates cannot be unbiased in their judgments. In fact, some of the very best judges and even plaintiff attorney's we know started their careers as defense attorneys. Unfortunately, many still show a certain amount of bias in favor of the insurance companies on some of our appraisals. It is no wonder because if you do get an Umpire on an appraisal who sides with the consumer on a significant dollar value claim, it is possible that he may never be suggested or approved again to serve as an umpire for that insurer without a court appointment. Also, most people do not realize how much insurance companies talk amongst themselves. Why would a person serving as an Umpire want to make a ruling that would have the effect of eliminating him from consideration on any future insurance related appraisal matters? Remember that this is how they make their living, so routinely ruling against insurance companies is the equivalent of biting the hand that feeds them. This elimination process is a significant disadvantage to a consumer looking to get fair treatment in the appraisal process, as the pool of qualified and unbiased Umpires is constantly being wilted down to just "their guys."

It is extremely difficult to find good, competent and unbiased appraisers and Umpires as a consumer, be they retired judges or professional mediators. The insurance industry has stacked the deck against the customer's efforts to get a fair resolution of their claims. The other problem with getting fair treatment in the appraisal process is one of the mindset of the Umpire. Most judges or mediators are used to the idea of reaching a compromise agreement between the parties. This usually means "splitting the baby." This is not a big deal if both you and the insurance company are both working from reasonable positions on the value of loss or if you are both working from very unreasonable positions. Unfortunately, all too often we go into this process with a realistic and honest evaluation, while the insurance company is stuck on an extreme low-ball estimate of damages. No matter how the Umpire splits the baby, the policyholder ends up with less than the fair value of his loss.

The way that appraisal is supposed to work is that the two appraisers each determine their loss evaluations separately and then meet to try to resolve their differences and reach an agreement on settlement of the appraisal. Any items that they cannot reach an agreement upon are to be submitted to the Umpire for his ruling one way or the other. This process is intended to set the value of the claim. Unfortunately, the latest trend is for the insurance company's appraiser to refuse to agree on any items with our appraiser, thus placing all items of damage in the Umpire's hands.

This significantly changes the entire appraisal process and usually leads to Umpires who assume control of the appraisal as if it they are still sitting on the bench as the judge. They exert a tremendous amount of influence in the appraisal, because both appraisers are afraid to offend him, which could lead to an unfavorable result for their nominator. Lately, we are seeing Umpires suggest their own compromise number somewhere in the middle of the two appraiser's evaluations and then they attempt to get one or the other of the parties to agree with their position. Remember, an agreement by any two of the three appraisers is a binding settlement of the claim. This process has evolved into most often a process of "splitting the baby."

It is for this reason that we are not big fans of appraisal to resolve a claim, generally speaking. We were taught that the appraisal was to be conducted as an open honest process of the two appraisers reaching agreements on as many line items as possible and then submitting the disputed items only to the Umpire. Then the Umpire was to make a judgment on which appraiser's position was the most correct given the loss situation. Today's appraisal process looks nothing like it was designed to be. It has been many years since we have had an Umpire actually take the time to go line by line through the appraiser's loss evaluations and decide the appraisal in this manner. Even though they are being paid by the hour, they seem all too happy to take the shortcut of compromising on an arbitrary number, without regard to the actual facts of the claim and how the values for each restoration operation were determined. Some even reject evaluations prepared on the Xactimate estimating software over a contractor bid, even though the courts in most jurisdictions have favored the software as the true fair value of the costs of restoration.

Notwithstanding all of these problems with appraisal, there are circumstances where appraisal is still the best means to reach a resolution of the claim and while it is far from a perfect process, it is still possible to get an acceptable result from appraisal even though the odds are stacked against you. The individual circumstances of each claim differ and dictate whether or not this process is the best strategy for a successful or at least an acceptable outcome.

Lately, we have seen a disturbing new trend by insurance companies whereby they may demand appraisal or agree to participate in an appraisal and then they try to limit what damages are the subject of appraisal and which cannot be ruled upon by the appraisal panel. You see under the rules of appraisal, issues that involve a question of the policy's coverage for damages are not within the scope of the appraisal process and these issues are strictly prohibited from being addressed by the appraisal panel. The appraisal process is designed to only determine the value of the loss in the event of a dispute.

It is extremely difficult in many cases to separate the value of the loss from what caused the damages. Insurance companies are trying to restrict the scope of the appraisal process by claiming that not all of the damages being claimed are the result of the covered loss being claimed. Because appraisers are not allowed in most jurisdictions to decide how the damages occurred, but only decide the value of the loss, this places the consumer at an unfair disadvantage by making the appraisal process irrelevant to resolving the dispute. Even after the appraisal is concluded, the consumer could still be forced to litigate the coverage issues on whether the damages claimed qualify for coverage under the policy. Using coverage as a tool, insurance companies can limit the scope of the appraisal and thus reduce the ultimate cost of the claim.

This issue on the authority of appraisers to address "causation" has been the source of recent litigation in Arizona and it has been addressed in other states as well with very different results. Arizona, which has a history of favoring alternative dispute resolutions methods, gives a certain amount of discretion to the appraisal panel to decide if the damages are the result of the covered loss. Yet, other states have more restrictive views on the authority of appraisers. If you encounter this situation, we suggest you find an experienced bad faith attorney who is familiar with the laws of your state.

Insurance companies are now using coverage issues, or more correctly, misusing coverage issues more and more often to limit the basis for the appraisal panel to make their loss determination and to obtain more favorable appraisal decisions. Insurance companies and their coverage attorneys are experts in separating you from your money. This practice is the second "D" as in Deny in the three "D's".

Your only other option in these situations is to take what you can get through appraisal or litigate your claim. Of course, litigation is not an easy process and it is not a quick resolution to your situation. Time is on the insurance companies' side, not yours. It can take 18 months or more to get your case before a jury on a bad faith insurance claim litigation. Not many people have the stamina and fortitude to make this trek and insurance companies know this, which is why this third "D" stands for Defend in their program.

Finding a qualified bad faith attorney to take on an insurance company for smaller dollar amounts can be very difficult if not impossible. This is why insurance companies seem more emboldened on the smaller claims. Hiring an attorney on an hourly basis is generally cost prohibitive unless you are independently wealthy, in which case you would probably not waste your time with this anyway. Attorney's fees on an hourly basis could easily exceed $50,000 by the time the case is ready for trial, not to mention the costs of experts and other litigation costs. The only reasonable option most people have is to find someone willing to handle their case on a contingency fee basis. But, as mentioned earlier, it is hard to find a good attorney to take on a claim with a small amount in dispute, as the cap on punitive damages that was imposed by the ruling in *Campbell* makes these cases unprofitable to litigate from a business standpoint.

Winning in litigation requires the perfect combination of facts, a very well-documented claim file, credible experts, a very experienced attorney, a tremendous amount of patience and a great deal of luck. Even if you win big, expect the insurance company to appeal the decision, so you go through another year or more and possibly another trial to get a final resolution to your claim. This is not an easy process and the deck is stacked against the policyholder. But, it is not impossible to persevere and get justice. We do it every day for our clients.

It is important to remember that most cases settle before trial. Most judges make a mediation mandatory before a case may proceed to trial. This alternative dispute method helps to give closure and finality to both sides in a disputed claim. Often the certainty of a mediated settlement, if it is enough is better than the uncertainty of an award by a jury. If your case is solid and well-prepared and if your attorney has done a good job of creating risk for the insurance company through discovery and through various motions to the court, there is a good chance that the insurance company's legal counsel will at some point in the litigation process recommend that the insurance company settle the case. Insurance companies know that most jurors are not sympathetic to insurance companies. If the plaintiff is perceived to be a good witness and the plaintiff attorney has created risk, a fair settlement is possible. Insurance companies are expert in evaluating risk. If your attorney does a good job of preparing your case through motions to the court, through great expert witnesses and through an extensive discovery process, it is likely that you can achieve a reasonable settlement sometime before trial.

There is one final alternative dispute method that we will not spend much time on, because it is rarely used in insurance disputes. This method is known as arbitration. Arbitration is a dispute resolution method that places the settlement in the control of a panel of arbitrators. A settlement under this process is final and binding upon the parties, which is generally not an attractive alternative to a courtroom in most cases. Submission of a claim dispute to arbitration is generally voluntary and happens only with the consent of the parties. In our 30 years in adjusting, we have had only a few cases submitted to arbitration, if that gives you a sense of how rare this method is used in insurance disputes on first party claims.

Not withstanding the above comments, there is a new trend in alternative dispute resolution alternatives. We are now seeing new policies with no appraisal clause in them but rather an arbitration provision. The one we have recently encountered in Iowa suggests that either party may suggest arbitrating the dispute, but that participation in arbitration is voluntary. If this is how your policy is worded get another policy immediately, as you will find that you are seriously limited in your options to pursue a fair settlement.

Whether your claim is resolved through appraisal or mediation, the result will likely be a compromise on what you believe to be the true value of your claim. Insurers will sometimes demand appraisal when they know they have exposure for damages, as this is a way of resolving the claim by paying less than the full value of loss. Consumers should avoid this process if at all possible, as it most often favors insurance companies. However, under the right circumstances, appraisal can provide a path to a practical resolution of your claim and in a reason amount of time.

Chapter Five

"But I Bought a Replacement Cost Policy?"

Insurance policies have evolved over the years from the simple "fire only" policies of the past into the more recent "Risks of Direct Loss" policies that are most common today. Insurance companies have expanded their policy coverages to meet consumer demands and increase premium revenues with these creative offerings. And what customer would not want full replacement cost recovery if they suffered a loss to their home or business. Yet, as the old saying goes, the devil is in the details.

While there are some replacement cost policies that pay the full replacement cost up front, these policies are rare and usually come at a significantly increased cost. The majority of "Full Replacement Cost" policies fall into a different category, because, while they do pay full replacement cost under a prescribed set of circumstances, there are hoops that you must jump through in order to obtain these policy benefits.

When you bought your policy, your insurance agent probably assured you that you were buying "Full Replacement Cost coverage for your home or business and your personal property. What he probably left out is that the insurance company is going to make you jump through all sorts of hoops in order to actually obtain these "Replacement Cost" policy benefits. We do not wish to cast doubt upon your agent's intentions, but the fact is, very few agents take the time to really explain to their customers how these replacement cost policies work at the time the policy is purchased. Most consumers discover for the first time after a loss event that certain steps must be taken to obtain the full replacement cost benefits suggested by the policy.

By up-selling consumers on replacement cost coverage, the insurance company earns an additional premium for the policy, and when customers are faced with the reality of what it takes to recover the full replacement cost for their claim, many are not willing to play the game and simply take what they can get without all the hoop jumping. Unfortunately, from our experience, very few claimants ever actually recover the full replacement cost policy benefits that are recoverable without professional assistance. Unless your claim is a total loss and you are significantly under-insured, it is unlikely that you will ever see the full replacement cost benefits that you were sold. There are those claims that the actual cash value of the loss exceeds the policy limits of coverage. In these cases, the limits of the coverage would be paid.

Many times we have reviewed insurance claims where the homeowner had driven all over town buying discounted building materials and negotiating with various subcontractors to get the very best price for repairs, only to find that all of their efforts only resulted in reducing the insurance company's obligation to them for the replacement cost benefits.

You might ask, "How is this possible? How can the insurer sell me a promise of replacement cost coverage and then give me something less?" The answer lies in the wording of the policy's "Loss Settlement" provision, which is where these hoops and qualifiers are located. Most of today's insurance policies contain stipulations in the Loss Settlement provision that restrict the insurance company's initial obligation for payment on the loss to the Actual Cash Value (ACV) of loss, until repair or replacement is completed. You may or may not know what the term Actual Cash Value means, but simply put, it is the depreciated value of the item lost or damaged after reductions for its current age and condition.

What this means is that you receive only the Actual Cash Value (depreciated) value payment up front and the insurance company withholds the depreciation portion until a receipt is produced proving the item is replaced.

On personal property coverage, most policies promise to settle the claim on a replacement cost basis, but for no more than the smallest of the following:

1. the actual cash value
2. the fair market value
3. the stated limit or other limit of insurance under this policy that applies to the property, or
4. the amount actually and necessarily spent to repair or replace damage to the property.

In other words, you only get the actual cash value, i.e., the depreciated value of the property, up front. If the actual amount spent is less than the replacement cost amount that was agreed to by the insurance company, you get the lesser of these amounts. It does not seem that complicated until you start replacing everything in your home or business and try to match up all the receipts with the listing of the personal property items and what happens when an item that is replaced is not exactly like the one that was destroyed? What if the items lost is no longer available for purchase? Will the insurance company allow me to substitute one item for another? These are just some of the reasons why very few homeowners ever receive the full policy benefits and this is why the policy is written this way.

To begin with the policy's requirements run directly in conflict with human nature. Everyone wants to get a good deal. Nobody wants to pay full retail price for something; they want to negotiate a discount; they want a deal. Negotiating may be good for buying a car, but on an insurance claim it may not ultimately benefit your situation. If you manage to negotiate a lower price with your contractor for repair of your home, the party that benefits from your efforts will probably be the insurance company. All you have done is spend your time and energy to lower the insurance company's obligation for payment of your claim.

Furthermore, insurance companies know that no one is going to replace every item in their home or business in the event of a major loss. So by structuring the replacement cost recovery in this manner, they can sell you replacement insurance coverage, at a higher premium, while rarely ever having to pay the full replacement cost policy benefits promised. Most agents do not explain what you must do in the event of a loss to obtain the replacement cost benefits of the policy when they sell you the policy. They just assure you that you have full replacement cost coverage. While this may be reassuring, it can be somewhat deceptive by omission.

We do not want to throw all of the good and well-meaning agents under the bus on this issue. Some of them may not truly understand how the policy is applied in a loss situation and one can argue that explaining every aspect of coverage to a customer before a loss is not reasonable when selling an insurance policy. But, by referencing their policies as a "replacement cost policies" the insurance companies are creating an expectation in consumers' minds that in reality are not exactly true. Maybe it would be better if they called these policies "qualifying replacement cost policies" so as to emphasize that a customer must take certain steps to obtain the replacement cost benefits. It would be more appropriate to make this provision known at the time their policy is sold. Instead, they hide the qualifying language deep within the dozens of pages of the policy. Or maybe insurers should place the replacement cost requirements at the front of the policy in bold sixteen-point type?

How is it possible that insurers are allowed to get away with this? The answer lies in the application of the law as it is applied in most courtrooms. Also, we can look to state statutes or to the regulations of the various state Departments of Insurance.

Under the law, the courts will generally interpret contract provisions by assigning them their plain and simple means. Unless the provision is subject to more than one reasonable interpretation or it violates some law, insurance contracts are generally given their strict meaning and construction by the courts. In other words, you are bound by the language in the policy unless you can prove that you were misled by the agent.

State statutory law is another place to look for modification to the insurance policy, as state statutes usually supersede the policy language. If you are lucky enough to live in a state that has a statute that requires the insurance company to pay the full replacement cost value of claim up front; regardless of the policy's verbiage, you may be entitled to receive the full replacement cost benefits of the policy. Also, if you live in a state that has a valued policy law and you have a qualifying total loss, you may be entitled to receive the full replacement cost benefits of the policy, without having to justify every expenditure.

Furthermore, state insurance regulatory agencies, usually referred to as the Department of Insurance, may exercise some regulatory control over the policy language and the language of all insurance coverage documents. In some states, before an insurer can issue a policy or revise a policy or insert a new policy provision, they must first get approval from the Department of Insurance. Unfortunately, many regulatory agencies, due in part to budget cuts, have gone to a policy of letting insurers write what they wish and they only step in if an issue of concern is brought to their attention. Many state agencies do not even review the policy documents; they just stamp them as received and file them, leaving the consumers to find their own remedies in the courtrooms.

Another condition that must be met in order to qualify for full replacement coverage on many policies is that the amount of insurance on the dwelling at the time of loss must equal or exceed the percentage stated under the building coverage's coinsurance percentage amount. This means that if the dwelling's replacement cost value at the time of loss is $100,000 and the coinsurance provision requires you to insure the dwelling to 80%, if your coverage limit on the dwelling is less than $80,000 you may incur a penalty, which is deducted from your claim proceeds. This issue is discussed more fully in a later chapter.

Also, under some of today's policies, certain types of property may not be eligible for replacement cost coverage. Items such as fences, decks, carpeting, awnings, household appliances, outdoor antennas and outdoor equipment are some of the types of items that are often covered only for their actual cash value, even under a replacement cost policy.

Finally, under most homeowners' policies, the insured may choose to settle the loss on an actual cash value basis and he may later make claim for the replacement cost value. Most policies require that the policyholder provide the insurance company notification of their intent to make claim for the replacement cost benefits within 180 days. While the policies are often silent as to how the 180-day period is calculated,

if at all possible we recommend using the date of loss as the trigger for this provision. This will help avoid trouble. If the claim goes on beyond the 180-day time limit before a settlement is reached, don't assume that you have forfeited your rights to the replacement cost recoveries. Make your claim immediately and if you get push back consult with an attorney, as many states have laws that toll (delay) these types of forfeiture provisions.

Additionally, most policies require that repairs or restoration be completed before the insurance company is obligated to issue payment. We are starting to see new policies that now include provisions that limit recovery for restorations completed to only restorations that are completed within 12 months of the date of loss. We have also seen policies that require repairs to be completed within two years. There are good legal arguments to be made and intervening factors to consider on how these policy provisions might be applied to your specific claim, but we would suggest that you try as much as possible to avoid problems by trying to work within the time frames allowed under your policy. Try as best you can to complete the restoration within the policy's required period. If that is not possible, write to the insurer asking for their written agreement to extend this time period. If they give you extra time, be sure that you have their agreement in writing. If they decline your request, consult with experienced insurance attorney to better understand your rights under the laws of your state.

The bottom line is that these policies provide full replacement cost coverage only if you incur this cost. So rather than run all over town trying to find ways to reduce your restoration costs, it might make more sense to use a qualified general contractor and let them do all the running for you. After all, that is what they are being paid for and you will not be entitled to these benefits anyway. So save yourself a lot of time and aggravation; hire a qualified professional and use the policy benefits to their full advantage. An insurance policy is not designed to put money in your pocket, but to restore you to the position you were in before the loss. At the end of the day that is what you should be striving for as well.

In recent weeks we have seen a new trend by insurance companies to withhold replacement cost claim benefits. You know, the benefits you paid extra for. They are now starting to demand the contractor's internal construction costs before they will pay the replacement cost benefits of the policy. You might ask how an insurer can obtain this private internal information on costs from a private party that is not a party to the insurance contract. A recent court ruling in Texas just answered that question for us, as this crazy judge actually supported the insurance company's position on the contractor's required production of his internal costs of construction on a client's home. Hopefully, this is an outlier rather than a judicial trend. As a public adjuster and former contractor, I do not see a reasonable basis under the law for the insurance company to demand and obtain a private company's confidential cost information. We will have to wait to see how this plays out for the next few years, as with one win under their belts, you can be assured that Insurers will keep pushing the envelope.

We have recently seen an increase in denials of coverage for repairs or personal property replacements that were not completed within the policy's stated time periods. Generally speaking, the courts have traditionally frowned upon these types of forfeiture clauses, but that has not stopped insurance companies from invoking these clauses to deny the full recovery of policy benefits. We recently had a major insurance company delay the consumer's first claim payment on their house fire for more than 9 months, and then when the restoration was completed on this total loss house fire, one year and three months after the date of loss, the insurance company refused to issue payment of the depreciation holdback on a replacement cost policy.

The English courts, as far back as the mid-17th century, created a rule of equity against the arbitrary forfeiture of contract rights under the theory that such forfeitures were unduly harsh. Our court system today, continues to disfavor such a draconian penalty as the forfeiture of insurance benefits in insurance contracts. While the policy sets forth specific limitations on the recovery of specific policy benefits, few courts will allow such a draconian penalty as the complete forfeiture of the contract benefits. The most prevalent legal theory is that of prejudice. Most courts in this situation will fall back on the concept of, how was the insurance company prejudiced by the delay in the claim submission for replacement cost benefits if the time goes beyond the policy's arbitrary date of forfeiture. If the insurer cannot show that they have been prejudiced in most jurisdictions they will not prevail.

Notwithstanding, if you can comply with the policy's time limits for making claim for replacement cost benefits, by all means make every attempt to do so. If the time period has expired and the insurance company refuses to accept the replacement cost claim, you should seek that advice of an insurance attorney, because there is a good chance of prevailing on this issue.

At this point you should be seeing how complex the job of adjusting an insurance claim is, especially for the average policyholder. This is why there is an entire industry that has developed to assist policyholders in fully recovering from their loss. Hiring a trained professional public adjuster may be your best insurance against the insurance industry's predatory claims handling activities. However, be careful. The wrong public adjuster can turn your claim into a nightmare just as quickly as the insurance company can. Don't rely solely on prior customer references, as these customers have no idea what they were entitled to on their claim. If the adjuster obtained a settlement that satisfied the customer, he will be a great source for testimonials. Unfortunately, he may have left thousands of dollars on the table, that neither he nor his customer knew about. At Skipton we say, Knowledge is power! Experience matters... as does education.

Chapter Six

Recovering Contractor's Overhead and Profit

We were recently contacted by a local restoration contractor who asked us if insurance companies are required to pay for contractor's overhead and profit on a claim settlement. The contractor had several claims with the same insurance company, but it had refused to pay the traditionally accepted contractor fees for Overhead and Profit (O&P), leaving him thousands of dollars short on these restoration projects. This is one of the more common deceptive claims practices that we encounter in our everyday claims handling.

It is not as if, at this point, there is any question about the fact that insurance companies are responsible for these legitimate contractor fees. Does the insurance company owe for contractor's overhead and profit on their building damages analysis? This issue has been addressed in courtrooms across the country on numerous occasions over the last two decades and the answers provided by the courts are a resounding YES!

This wrongful claim practice of not paying contractor overhead and profit was addressed by the court as far back as 1982 in the Arizona Supreme Court case of *Zuckerman vs. Transamerica Ins. Co.* Although that case's dispute originated over the O&P issue, it was the forfeiture clause which was eventually brought before the Supreme Court. However, the court did address the O&P issue via former Supreme Court Justice Feldman's specific footnote on page 141, marked by ** which states: *"The company's (Transamerica's) position is dubious on this point. The policy contains no clause permitting such deductions from the amount of loss. It does provide that the company "does ensure" Zuckerman "to the extent of the actual cash value of the property..." (Emphasis supplied.)*[13]

But insurance companies can be very persistent when it comes to reducing claims payments and increasing profits. So this again became an issue in 1994, in a class action lawsuit that was filed in Pennsylvania over State Farm's practice of routinely deducting amounts for contractor overhead & profit, in addition to depreciation from their replacement cost estimates to determine the actual cash value claim payment. The court in *Gilderman v. State Farm Ins.*, 649 A.2d 941 (Pa. Super. 1994) ruled as follows: *"We hold that repair or replacement costs include any cost that an insured is reasonably likely to incur in repairing or replacing a covered loss."*[14]

This reasoning was followed a few years later in the state of Michigan in *Salesin v. State Farm Fire & Cas.*[15] Since that time, this issue has been subject to class action lawsuits in several other jurisdictions,

including Texas and Oklahoma. This issue was also the subject of discussion in an August 2000 insurance industry article written in Claims magazine. In this article, the author laid out the reasoning behind inclusion and exclusion of contractor O&P payments under an insurance policy. The author concludes that insurance adjusters should consider the circumstances as outlined in the *Gilderman* and *Salesin* courts' rulings, stating: "Under this view, overhead and profit are assumed to have gone into the property when it was new. The insured is considered to have some of that value left at the time of loss, and loss of that value should be considered part of the damage suffered by the insured."[16]

In 2006, the Arizona Court of Appeals ruled in *Tritschler v. Allstate* as follows: *"… if the cost to repair or replace the damaged property would likely require the services of a general contractor, the contractor's overhead and profit fees should be included in determining actual cash value, even when an insured ultimately elects to complete personally the needed repairs."*[17]

And just recently, the Florida Supreme Court in its July 2013 decision in *Trinidad v. Florida Peninsula*[18] left no doubt that this wrongful reduction of policy benefits will not be tolerated in Florida. The court ruled that homeowners are entitled to recover the full cost of replacement, whatever that includes, and whether or not the repair or reconstruction actually takes place.[19]

You might ask yourself, with similar rulings like these all over the country, why would insurance companies continue to engage in this wrongful claims handling practice? The answer is simple; it is all about the money. With a 20% savings on every claim payout, the money is just too enticing for many insurance companies. Insurance companies count on the fact that most people do not know their rights under an insurance policy, so they are easy marks for being short changed in their purchase of an insurance policy. And because most people do not seek professional help when they have a claim, they are left to rely upon the integrity of their insurance company.

Insurance companies are meant to do an actuarial analysis to try to make their money by taking policy premium payments in exchange for a promise of coverage should a covered loss event happen. Insurance companies keep careful records of past loss events and they are quite good at predicting future events as well. These actuarial records are not only effective for predicting the number of loss events in a given year, they are also effective for analyzing the insurer's exposure to liabilities created by the filing of a lawsuit. It is a fact that very few claimants will go to the trouble and the expense of hiring an attorney if they feel they are being treated unfairly on a claim. Some estimate this number to be much less than 5% of all claimants. Also, of the few claimants who choose to sue, less than 5% of them will ever see the inside of a courtroom, as the majority will settle sometime before trial.

To better explain how this tactic works, let's put some hypothetical numbers to this theory, so as to get a better understanding of how this all works. For the purposes of this example, let's assume that an insurer will suffer 1,000 fire claims in a given year with an average sized claim of $100,000 before application of contractor's O&P; this means that, on average, if the insurer does not pay contractor's O&P, it will save a total of $20,000 (or 20%) of the damages per claim.

If this insurance company refuses to pay contractor's overhead & profit on all of these claims, we can assume that a certain number of customers will not take this laying down and will file suit against the insurer. Using the litigation probability data from past experience, this means that less than 5% of the claimants, or approximately 50 of them, will actually file suit against the insurance company. Of these,

less than 5% will actually stay in all the way to a jury trial, meaning that there will only be 2 or 3 trials that result from such blatantly wrongful conduct.

Remember, the US Supreme Court's ruling in *Campbell* reduced the penalties for getting caught for intentional bad faith claims practices to a factor of a single digit multiplier of the contract damages claimed, i.e. less than 10 times. So here, the claimant's contract damages average $20,000. Using the *Campbell* ruling as a guideline, the most that the court can award for punitive damages is $180,000 or 9 times the contract damages, plus, of course, the $20,000 that it should have paid in the first place.

Assuming that the insurance company loses all three (3) trials, its exposure is a total of just $540,000 in punitive damages, plus the contract damages it should have paid in the beginning, of $60,000.

Now, let's compare this payout to the money the insurance company would have saved on all of the other claims where it withheld contractor's overhead & profit. There were 950 of the 1,000 claimants that did not file a lawsuit, but instead stood by and took what was offered to settle their claim. On these claims the insurance company saved $19,000,000; yes that is right...$19 million dollars.

Then there are the other 47 people who filed a lawsuit but settled their cases before trial. For these claimants, let's assume that their attorneys were successful in getting the insurance company to pay the contractor's overhead & profit and they got them to pay an additional $20,000 for the attorney's fees and costs. These costs would total $940,000, plus the wrongfully withheld amounts, totaling another $940,000.

To summarize, the net savings for the insurance company engaged in this blatantly improper conduct is roughly $16.5 million dollars. The math works as follows: there was the initial $20,000 per claim withheld, that the insurance company eventually was forced to pay on the 50 claims that filed suit, which totals $1 million. Now add to this the extra settlement costs for the 47 people who settled their claims before litigation; this totals approximately another $940,000. Lastly, we must add the amount's awarded in the 3 trials that resulted from this wrongful conduct which total, $540,000. So in doing the math, we have $1M, plus $940k, plus $540K for a total insurer cost of $2,480,000. This example only considered 1,000 claims. Imagine how much money is at stake when you apply this practice to the actual number of claims that an insurance company handles each year.

If we were to give you $19 million dollars, would you be willing to give us $2.5 million of it back? Only paying out to those who recognize that this practice is wrong can certainly pay huge dividends. There can be no other explanation for the same insurance company that has lost on this issue in the courts to still be engaging in this wrongful claims practice. And it is even clearer now why that company is one of those in the top ten of the Consumer Reports[20] listing of the worst insurance companies.

When your insurance company sends its loss evaluation to you, you need to look at the last couple of pages to see if they have included contractor's overhead & profit in their evaluation. To help you better understand what to look for, please see *figure #1* below which shows a properly calculated loss evaluation. Then compare it to *figure #2* which shows how insurers often times prepare their loss evaluations to exclude the contractor overhead & profit costs they should be paying.

Summary for Dwelling			
Line Item Total			954,188.74
Total Adjustments for Base Service Charges			789.10
Material Sales Tax	@	9.446%	28,377.88
Storage Rental Tax	@	9.446%	25.28
Subtotal			983,381.00
Overhead	@	10.0%	98,338.10
Profit	@	10.0%	98,338.10
Replacement Cost Value			$1,180,057.20
Less Depreciation			(133,843.12)
Actual Cash Value			$1,046,214.08
Net Claim			$1,046,214.08
Total Recoverable Depreciation			133,843.12
Net Claim if Depreciation is Recovered			$1,180,057.20

Figure #1 – Depicts the correct manner of preparing a loss evaluation[21]

Summary for Dwelling

Line Item Total			693,843.50
Sales Tax Prime Cont	@	6.140%	42,601.99
Replacement Cost Value			**$736,445.49**
Less Depreciation			(113,360.11)
Actual Cash Value			**$623,085.38**
Less Deductible			(5,000.00)
Net Claim			**$618,085.38**
Total Recoverable Depreciation			113,360.11
Net Claim if Depreciation is Recovered			**$731,445.49**

*Figure#2 – Depicts the improper exclusion
of contractor overhead and profit*

As you can see from these two examples, the exclusion of contractor's overhead & profit makes a significant impact on the total amount of a claim recovery. And it significantly impacts the insurance company's bottom line.

In the interests of full disclosure, there is a recent case in Pennsylvania that has revisited the *Gilderman* overhead and profit issue and has watered down the original ruling somewhat. Let's just say that the overhead and profit issue seems to be an issue that will likely see more court time in the future.

In fact, some insurers are taking steps to change their policies coverage language so as to justify not paying contractor profit and overhead. We recently ran across a Farmer's policy with an endorsement #7122 which essentially states that they do not pay for contractor's overhead and profit or building permits or architect charges, until they are actual "incurred" and submitted for payment.

As I thought about this endorsement, it dawned on me that Arizona is a statutory policy state, meaning that the legislature enacted a law that requires all policy's in the state to conform to the minimum standards of coverage set forth in the New York Standard Fire Policy of 1943.

What this means that that no policy can be written that does not, as a minimum conform to this policy. In looking to the Standard

Fire Policy, there is clearly no basis for the reduction of overhead and profit from the actual cash value payment that is required under most policies. I gave this idea for one of my attorneys who successfully used in in a litigation case on this issue. The judge in that case ruled in our favor stating that this endorsement is not enforceable in the state of Arizona. Notwithstanding this ruling, Farmer's continues to use this endorsement on their policy's, as we have only recently encountered is again on a commercial policy.

Knowledge is power! Knowing the law is an important aspect to representing consumers on insurance claims. There are currently 29 states that have adopted the Standard Fire policy, but be careful, as the manner in which they have adopted the Standard fire policy can be different than how the Arizona legislature did it. Some states have only adopted it with respect to fire losses, so a windstorm claim would be not be applicable or achieve same result.

This is not the only way that insurers squeeze out extra profits from your claim. Be sure to double check the math on their loss evaluations, as it is not uncommon for an insurance company to pay contractor's overhead & profit on only certain portions of the claim, rather than on the entirety of the loss.

We often encounter insurers who calculate contractor overhead & profit, excluding some of the repairs that are called out in their evaluations. On an active litigation matter, we found an insurer who had excluded the cost of roofing from its calculation of contractor overhead & profit. Their explanation for this reduction thus far has been somewhat murky, but with critical depositions in the next couple of weeks, we will likely flush out that explanation.

Contractor's overhead & profit numbers are not the only omissions that we routinely find on insurance company loss evaluations. Other typical exclusions include some of the other contractor services that are required to complete the restoration of your property, such as building permits, crane rental, residential or commercial supervision and environmental remediation (asbestos).

One of the insurance industry's favorite practices is to exclude the payment of contractor's overhead & profit on the payment for the cost of building permits. If your adjuster has done this on your claim, suggest that he drive downtown to the City's Building and Planning Department and sit in the waiting area for the plans check desk for hours to get the building permit issued to begin reconstruction. It is absurd to believe that this task does not require significant time and effort and do not be fooled by his explanation that this costs is included with the payment of overhead & profit on the other portion of the claim. In the restoration estimating software known as Xactimate, which is the most widely used insurance estimating tool, there is a button that you can click which provides a detailed explanation of exactly what services are included in the line-item description. For the line item pertaining to the cost of obtaining a building permit, contractor's overhead & profit should be paid as an addition cost, to compensate the contractor for his time in obtaining the proper permits.

Likewise, insurance companies sometimes exclude contractor's overhead & profit from the costs for the rental of a crane or other heavy equipment. Simply put, why should the contractor spend his time securing the necessary heavy equipment to make the repairs and not receive compensation for his time?

Another trade that is most often excluded from contractor's overhead & profit is asbestos or mold abatement. It is quite common for insurers to exclude this cost, primarily because these costs can be very high and they require the services of a properly trained and licensed abatement contractor. If the general contractor has any involvement with the hiring or scheduling of the abatement contractor, it is entirely proper to pay the general contractor for his overhead & profit on the abatement work.

Another area that has been the target of insurance's cost cutting efforts in residential or commercial supervision. This line item is designed for the time a general contractor must have a supervisor on the contraction site to oversee the work, schedule the work, meet with the building inspectors and be certain that all OSHA required safety protocols and being adhered to. Because this is truly an estimated cost based upon experience, something most insurance adjusters do not have, this is an easy line items for the insurance company to challenge. The insurance adjusters take the position that these costs should be covered under the general contractor's overhead and profit. But, a quick review of the "white paper" in Xactimate, makes it clear that these are extra charges for work not including in any of the loss evaluation's line items.

These are just some of the more common examples of the manipulations that insurance companies so often make when determining the actual cash value of a claim. There are as many potential wrongful reductions to your loss evaluation as there are creative claims adjusters and claims managers. The key is to be diligent in reviewing the claim evaluation and hold your insurance company accountable for the full value of your loss.

Chapter Seven

Misapplication of Depreciation

The use of depreciation can significantly impact the consumers' ultimate recovery for their loss, just as the intentional misuse of depreciation can. This is one of those areas of insurance that is so complex that many insurance adjusters do not even truly understand the proper methods for determining the correct amount to depreciate your property. So then, how can a consumer know whether or not they are being treated fairly by the insurance company in the settlement of their claim? Add to this, the fact that even knowing how to use depreciation properly still leaves a great deal that is subject to opinion or speculation and you have created a system that encourages abusive claims handling practices.

It is a fact that the improper use of depreciation is one of the most abused of all the insurance claim processes. It is likely this way because the subjective nature of applying depreciation insulates the insurance company significantly from claims of bad faith claims handling conduct. This is because it can be extremely difficult to prove that the adjuster's application of excessive depreciation to the damaged property was intentionally designed to underpay the claim and not just a mistake in judgment. Not to get too into the legal processes that govern insurance bad faith law, generally speaking, if a consumer wishes to file litigation against an insurance company alleging bad faith claims handling, he must prove that the insurance company was deliberate in their abuse of the valuation process and not simply mistaken or grossly negligent. This can be difficult to prove on something that is as subjective as the application of depreciation to damaged real property or business/personal property items.

Also, because consumers are not trained in the proper application of depreciation and because the methods used are not actually spelled out in the policy, it is nearly impossible for a consumer to know if they are being mistreated. This not knowing the proper application of depreciation increases the likelihood that the misuse of the depreciation valuation process will become epidemic. The fact is that in most claims that we are asked to review, insurers left on their own appear to apply excessive amounts of depreciation to both structure losses and on personal property items.

You might ask why an insurance company would do this. The answer is elementary; the less money that they pay out initially, the less ability that the consumer has to replace all of their damaged property. And the more hoops they erect to discourage recovery of this additional depreciation holdback indemnity, the less likely the customers will be to make these claims. The fact is; these policy provisions are cleverly constructed to give the insurance company the upper hand and to improve their corporate net profits. They know that no one will replace everything in their home or business in the event of a major loss. And what you don't replace, you lose the depreciation holdback on.

You are sold an insurance policy with assurances that it includes full replacement cost coverage; yet most claimants never get the full benefits of the policy's promise of coverage. As mentioned in the previous chapter, we believe that this process defies the policyholders' reasonable expectations of insurance coverage and we do not believe that an insurer should be allowed to sell a replacement cost policy without making it crystal clear to the buyer the exact terms of the replacement agreement.

Depreciation is applicable to both your personal and business property as well as to your real property (buildings). The rules of application are essentially the same for both real property and personal property. Depreciation is designed to account for the age of an item, the use of the property and the possible obsolescence of the property damaged, to create a current street value for the items as they were at the time of the loss. This is what is referred to as the actual cash value of the property. There are three primary tests for the measurement of actual cash value used by the courts. Which test your state uses is something you will need to find out through your own research or through the help of attorney.

In some jurisdictions, the actual cash value of property is defined as replacement cost less depreciation, which is the current replacement cost of the damaged item, minus a depreciation amount to account for the age and wear and tear of the item.

Other states recognize "fair market value" as the test of actual cash value. Fair market value is defined as the price that property would realize in a marketplace of willing buyers and sellers, acting in their own interests, within a reasonable period of time. In those states that recognize this method for determination of actual cash value, this method has produced mixed results and confusion, primarily due to the differences between the application of this method by state law and the methods set forth in most insurance contracts which define actual cash value as replacement cost less depreciation. There have been instances where creative insurance companies have been able to use fair market value laws to exploit the valuation process to the detriment of their policyholders.

The majority of state courts in the United States recognize the "Broad Evidence Rule" as the standard by which insurers are to determine the cash value of destroyed property. Under the Broad Evidence Rule, an insurance company cannot rely solely upon the two traditional methods of *market value* or *replacement cost value minus depreciation* as the exclusive methods for value determination. Under the Broad Evidence Rule, these traditional methods can be used as a guideline, but the insurance company must give due consideration to every fact and circumstance that would logically lead to a correct value of the damaged or destroyed property. This rule requires that a thorough examination be made of every standard of value that might have a bearing on the property being considered. Some of these standards include; the age of the item, the use factor, the obsolescence of the property, the profit likely to accrue from the property, the property's tax value, the replacement cost, the condition of the property, the location, the market value, the original cost, offers for buy or sell, etc.

Then there are a few states that have not weighed in definitively as to the recognized method for determining actual cash value. While state laws vary on the methods of valuation, most insurance companies use the method set forth in the insurance policy of replacement cost value minus depreciation to determine the actual cash value payments. It has been our experience that nearly all insurance companies consider only the useful life (age) of the items in making their determination of value, even in the states that follow the Broad Evidence Rule. Few insurers take into consideration the type of property being evaluated and most have very punishing and often unreasonable depreciation schedules.

We have seen insurers taking 60% depreciation on a 6 year old set of metal storage shelves. In our off-site file storage, we have metal shelving that we bought more than 20 years ago that still works just as they did the day we bought them. We have had insurance companies depreciate a 100 year old antique oak desk by 90%. Antiques by their nature, generally do not go down in value as they get older, but in fact become even more valuable with age. This is the nature of an antique. On other occasions, we have seen insurers apply depreciation to items that were new and unopened at the time of loss, simply because an insured listed the item as 6 months old, such as Christmas presents purchased early.

In the insurance industry's claims training textbooks, adjusters are trained to use the broad evidence rule in making their determination of actual cash values. One such textbook, Property Loss Adjusting by James Markham[22] gives an example of how the use of a sofa can affect its' value. In this example, the author explains that a 5 year old sofa in the living room of a family with 6 kids and a dog would probably show far more wear than the same sofa in the living room of an elderly retired couple.

This same criteria can be applied to a 3 year old men's business suit. If it is worn by a banker who wears suits every day for work, it is likely to exhibit far more wear than a suit owned by a retired gentlemen who only wears a suit once or twice a year to special functions. In this scenario, the older gentlemen's suit could easily last ten or fifteen years and would surely not depreciate as quickly as the banker's suit.

Notwithstanding this training that adjusters should have received and the state laws that regulate property valuation, insurers use punishing depreciation schedules that are designed to significantly underpay the actual cash value of the damaged property. This is probably the most prominent deceptive claims practices that we encounter. The insurance industry does not consider the use of your property or the condition at the time of loss. They base their loss evaluations upon archaic depreciation schedules that were never designed for application to property insurance claims valuation and which significantly understate the useful life of the damaged property, such as various government depreciation tables. They then rely upon the age of the items as the sole determination of the current actual cash value. These depreciation table were designed as an accounting treatise for tax purposes, not for insurance claims.

To better illustrate how this might affect the average homeowner, let's assume that you had a total loss house fire and that the total replacement cost value of your personal property was $150,000.00. It is not uncommon for an insurance company, using heavy-handed deprecation to value your personal property at 50% or less of its' current replacement cost value. You are left with $75,000 to replace $150,000 worth of property. This places a very heavy burden upon you, the property owner, to try to repurchase all of this property, submit replacement receipts for the depreciation holdback and wait for their check so that they can go buy more items and submit more receipts and on and on until you just get tired and give up.

The fact is; no one will repurchase all of their destroyed items, which is exactly why the insurance industry set up the game in this manner. Again, they sell you the illusion of replacement cost coverage, but erect barriers to assure that you never actually receive the full benefits of the policy.

The insurance company's adjuster will never tell you this, but you do not have to replace each and every item with exactly the same item. Provided that the items serve the same purpose, it should qualify as a reasonable replacement item. For instance, let's say you lost a sofa in your family room, but would rather replace it with two reclining chairs instead. That substitution should be meet with no resistance from the insurance company.

Turning our attention to the application of depreciation on real property, i.e. your home or commercial building, insurance companies follow the same patterns in their application of depreciation to building items. We recently had an insurance company take 30% depreciation on the plumbing system of a 5-year-old home that was a total loss from a fire. Using this depreciation schedule, my client' plumbing, according to the insurance company, would have only had a 20-year useful life expectancy.

On this same claim, they took 28% on their windows, 35% on their wood burning stove and 23% on the heating/air conditioning ductwork. By the time they got finished, they had taken an 18% overall depreciation of this 5-year-old structure. To suggest that a home's useful life expectancy is only 30 years is ridiculous. We know of many homes from our home neighborhood that were built in about 1955 that are in as good condition today as they were then. And they have never had to replace their plumbing or the heating ductwork.

The application of excessive depreciation is rampant. The most common and heavily depreciated items are floor coverings and paint. These items do actually depreciate faster than other building components, but rarely at the rates that we commonly see used by the insurance companies. Most adjusters do not inquire as to when you last painted your house and often use arbitrary values that have no relationship to the actual condition of the paint at the time of loss.

Another trick that is commonly used by insurance company adjusters is to depreciate repair items. The rules that guide the practice of insurance adjusters dictates that repairs are not subject to depreciation, because you are not replacing the item, only fixing it. The adjuster training textbooks suggest that when trying to explain depreciation to a consumer that they explain it in terms of betterment. For instance, if you have a 10-year-old roof, with a life expectancy of 20 years, if it gets destroyed in a windstorm, the fair value of the roof at the time of loss was 50% of the current replacement value based upon its' age at the time of loss. The consumer is made better by the fact that they got a new roof for an older roof and when the 10-year- old roof would have worn out, they have now gained 10 more years of useful life on the replacement roof.

What we commonly see in practice is insurance companies taking depreciation on the repair of a roof. Let's say that the insurer agrees to replace one slope of the roof. All too often, we find them taking depreciation on this partial replacement, which is actually a repair, not a replacement at all.

Another common trick is taking depreciation on partial repairs of framing. Assume your home had a fire loss that burned 6 of the 30 roof trusses that make up your roof system. Many insurers put replacement of the roof trusses in their evaluations and then apply depreciation to the replacement trusses. Thinking back to the term betterment, will the consumer be made better if 6 of his 30 trusses are new? When the rest of the house falls down from decay in 200 years, will these 6 trusses still be standing? Under the concept of betterment, the consumer has received no betterment by the replacement of these 6 roof trusses.

The list goes on and on. We see drywall repairs from water damage, where the insurer agrees to cut out the bottom 2 feet of drywall around the room that was water damaged and then they apply depreciation to the new drywall repairs. We often see exterior siding repairs depreciated in a similar manner.

One explanation for the insurance adjuster's misunderstanding of the proper application of depreciation is because most insurance companies have gone to relatively abbreviated training programs. It is not uncommon for a major insurance company to have a two, three or four week adjuster training program. You simply cannot train an insurance adjuster in 2 to 4 weeks to any reasonable level of competence.

Another reason for the misapplication of depreciation is their lack of training added to the computer software program's terminology. When using Xactimate, if you were to estimate the water damages repair mentioned above, you would enter into the computer system "Replace." Then if you are replacing the drywall perimeter of the room up to the two foot height, you would calculate the number of square feet and enter this number into the system. While the system says that you are replacing, let's say 90 square feet of drywall, this is not a replacement of drywall that is a depreciable event.

The fact is; a partial replacement of a building component is considered a repair and not a replacement by the insurance industry. It has been this way for decades, at least until recently. Partial repairs are not subject to depreciation, period. If you find your insurance company applying excessive depreciation or depreciating partial repairs, call them out on it. Fight back, because the facts are in your favor. Ask them to provide a written explanation for their application of depreciation to your loss and do not allow them to depreciate a repair. Think logically and put your arguments in writing. If they apply 35% depreciation to paint to a room you had repainted just a year ago, put it to them in writing and make them revise their position or justify it. A quick internet search will help you find many good articles to support this position.

Chapter Eight

What if the Expert is wrong?

We recently had a claim on a commercial cabinet shop that was burned in the middle of the night by an act of arson. The evidence revealed that there were at least 26 different points of origin, meaning that there were 26 fires set within the building. The owners, Chuck and Therese, had played by the rules, and they spent a decade building their business into one of the premier custom cabinet shops in the southwest. Their work was highly acclaimed, and they had received numerous awards for excellence in their craftsmanship and for their business success.

But, the insurance company's adjuster, upon finding that the fires were intentionally set and knowing the economic troubles of the 2008 recession, immediately decided that Chuck and Therese must have set this fire themselves, probably because their business was not doing well. The insurance company then retained a CPA/expert to comb through every personal and business financial record they could find, in an attempt to find some financial problems that they could use to show that Chuck and Therese were motivated to intentionally burn down their own business.

After months of highly invasive inquiries into their lives, the insurance company's CPA/expert, being truly unable to find a real financial motive, authored a report suggesting that they might have burned their building down, because they could rent a similar size building for much less than their current mortgage payment. Even the motivated insurance company could not buy into this absurd theory and finally began issuing small claim payments.

The fact is that Chuck and Therese were very responsible business people who did not owe on anything other than their commercial building and their home mortgages. They had a nice savings account and their business, even though down slightly during the recession, was poised to have a banner year with the recession in the rearview mirror, and more than a million dollars in new orders for the coming year. Throughout the insurance company's investigation, its representatives all ignored Chuck and Therese's belief that the fire was set by a recently fired employee. The insurance company had decided Chuck and Therese were guilty and all of its efforts were focused on proving that, so as to avoid payment of their claim.

Unfortunately, by the time the insurance company's investigation was completed and nominal payments finally were issued, it was too late to save their business. All of their 27 employees had taken other jobs, because they could not go without paychecks for the four months that the investigation took to complete. And because the insurance company refused to provide any financial assistance until its investigation was complete, Chuck and Therese had no money to set up a temporary shop to remake their pending jobs. Hence, they lost existing orders and no one was interested in a bid on a new job from a shop that was currently out of business, thereby causing further economic losses.

But to add insult to injury, the CPA/expert retained by the insurance company had the audacity to take Chuck and Therese's actual accountant-prepared profit & loss statements and revise their actual earnings downward in a blatant attempt to under-value their loss of business income. In litigation, our financial expert said that he had never seen a CPA revise actual P&L statements of a business in this manner and he was deeply critical of the suggestion by the insurance company's CPA that his modified P&L statements reflected the actual earnings of the business. Of course, using these artificially depressed numbers as the basis for projecting future revenues caused a huge reduction in the insurance company's calculation of lost business income. In the end, these issues of bias and wrongdoing were exposed and a significant seven figure settlement was agreed upon. But, even a large settlement like this could not restore Chuck and Therese's reputation or their financial position before the fire loss. The insurance company abandoned them in their darkest hour, using its experts against them in an attempt to save money on payment of their claim.

Changes in the way insurance companies handle claims over the last decade has spawned an exponential growth in the expert/consultant industry. Traditionally, an expert was a master craftsman, a practicing engineer, architect, doctor, or accountant. Such experts were often practicing professionals in their fields who could be called upon to provide expertise on questions within their field of knowledge and training. But, today, an entire industry of experts has evolved from working professionals to firms designed primarily to provide insurance companies with expert opinions on a variety of claims issues, from the causation of damages to the method of repairs to the value of the claim. Engineers, roofing consultants, accountants, and others provide their "expert" opinions on many questions of fact that arise in the processing of insurance claims.

For instance, your roof might have been damaged by a violent hailstorm, causing you to make a claim to your insurance company. Your insurance company responds by sending an adjuster to inspect the damages. If the claims process works as it was initially designed, the adjuster confirms the damages, prepares a loss evaluation and issues payment for your claim. Sadly, there are very few insurance companies today who still process claims in this manner.

Most insurance companies have removed all discretion from the front- line adjuster, and instead, the claims manager now micro-manages the claim from a desk thousands of miles away. Often, the adjuster will tell us that he has been instructed to have the damages inspected by an "expert." Most often, the adjuster does not choose the expert; rather it is the insurance company that chooses what expert will be conducting inspections on their behalf. None of what we have discussed is unreasonable or improper, provided that the expert is truly an expert in the field required and provided that he or she is fair, honest and unbiased in all determinations.

Unfortunately, all too often lately, the insurance companies choose an "expert" or "consultant" who has little or no real training in the field of knowledge required and who is not operating as an unbiased expert, giving a factual report to the insurance company on the issues being investigated. We routinely find architects or civil engineers investigating damages that are beyond the scope of their training and expertise. Many operate under the umbrella of large national engineering firms that provide credibility for their opinions. You see, in the engineering world, it is considered proper for any engineer or architect in the firm to conduct field investigations for the firm and they can then produce an engineering report that is signed and stamped by an engineer in the firm who is licensed in the state where the claim arises.

In a recent large commercial claim, an architect was brought in before our involvement, and he wrote a report saying there was no hail damage to the roofs. These types of reports are all too common. Indeed, following the 2010 hail storm in Phoenix, we saw literally dozens of these types of reports, suggesting there were no hail damages; yet we recovered on virtually all of these claims. In this particular case, the consumer was referred to our firm and we notified the insurance company that we intended to conduct an inspection with an engineer, and we invited the insurance company to participate. The insurer responded with a civil engineer for the same engineering firm, and we took the time to research that person prior to our scheduled meeting. At our meeting, we informed her that we had checked her background and the civil engineering curriculum from the university where she obtained her degree, and we found no coursework or other training on roofing systems that would qualify her as an expert on hail damages to roofing materials. She admitted that she had no formal training other than her on-the-job experience, for which she had only been on the job for less than a year, yet this was the person the insurance company was relying upon to decide if there were covered damages to the policyholder's roofs.

She attended the site inspection, telling us that she was only instructed to observe our engineer's investigation. Despite multiple offers, she refused to actively engage in a joint investigation with our engineers. Our engineer would ask her technical questions to determine her level of competence, which she would refuse to answer. These questions caused her to spend much of her time, while we were doing our investigation, walking around the rooftops and taking an occasional picture. To our surprise, three weeks after this site meeting, we received a thirty-eight page engineering report authored by her, mimicking the architect's previous report and concluding that there were no hail damages to these roofs. This matter was recently resolved when a panel of three independent appraisers awarded the policyholder more than a million dollars for his damages.

This situation raises the question: "How is it that three independent damage appraisers were able to confirm hail damages to these roofs, when two insurance company experts, an engineer, and an architect, all found there to be no damage?" The answer is both simple and disturbing. Many insurance companies are using experts with only a slight degree of familiarity in the subject matter, and they are often engaging biased experts who are willing to "sell" favorable opinions of fact to insurance companies.

As discussed earlier in this book, a tremendous amount of pressure has been exerted on claims departments to hold down the costs of claims. Remember, the less the insurance company pays out in claims, the more profit is retained for the company. So the temptation is simply too great for some insurance companies to not engage in these deceptive practices. And, because it is so difficult to prove intentional wrongdoing, there is little to lose and much to gain from such a program.

Due to the substantial amounts of money involved in providing expert services to insurance companies, there is no shortage of "experts" willing to participate in this process. After all, if an insurance company can save more than a million dollars, as they tried to do on the claim referenced above, it is worth spending a few thousand dollars on an expert report.

Recently, we have come to know a local engineer through our claims work where he was the insurance company's designated expert. On two different claims we have encountered him deliberately hiding evidence that did not support his opinions. These documents were obtained through the legal discovery process and showed that on one instance, he knew that there was a hailstorm with 1.75 inch hail, because the report was in his file, but he completely ignored it and took the position that there was only minor damage that was from a prior hailstorm.

On another occasion, he ignored the fact that the insurance company had retained another engineer to assess the damages from hail, to which they confirmed hail damages to the policyholder's building. He made a file note stating (mistakenly) that since the first engineers report was never sent to the policyholder, he was not going to reveal it. He went on to write his report completely ignoring the initial engineering report and he took the position that there was no damage to the property from hail.

The obvious question you are probably asking is, "Are you saying that there are insurance companies that are telling their experts to mislead the public in their reports?" The answer generally is NO! These experts understand the process without instruction. They know what answers the insurance company is looking for and because the insurance company is their customer, (often a very large customer), they want to satisfy their customer's needs. In these situations, their needs, often, are not the truth, but a predetermined conclusion that will save the insurance company substantial money in claims payments. The insurance companies do not need to micromanage these experts; rather, they can achieve the same result by simply removing unwilling or uncooperative "experts" from their approved vendor list.

It may come as a surprise to most insurance consumers, but this corrupt process of insurance company's using biased experts has been well-documented. Just such a practice was at the center of a class-action lawsuit in Oklahoma in 2006 that resulted in a $13 million dollar verdict for the plaintiffs.[23] This lawsuit alleged that a major insurance company hired a Texas-based engineering firm, which intentionally undervalued damage to homes and/or claimed that the damage was caused by other factors, such as faulty construction, rather than tornado damage. According to a CNN report, "The jury ruled that [the insurance company] 'recklessly disregarded' its duty to deal fairly and act in good faith with the [insureds] and that it 'intentionally and with malice' breached its duties as the couple's insurance company." "The jury further found 'clear and convincing evidence' that [the insurance company] recklessly disregarded its duty to act fairly and in good faith with members of the class action by employing [the engineering firm] and its independent adjusters...."

The same engineering firm was also involved in a 2006 investigation by the Attorney General of the State of Mississippi over its alleged wrongdoing in preparing damage reports for the same insurance company on hundreds of homeowner's claims from Hurricane Katrina[24]. In this incident, two sisters who supervised claims handlers for the insurer served as whistleblowers to expose how the insurance company's adjusters manipulated engineering reports to change the cause of damage from wind (a covered cause of loss) to storm surge (not covered by insurance company's policy) so as to deny coverage for legitimate claims.

This same engineering firm was at the center of another case where it was alleged that the insurance company knowingly used a biased consulting report to deny coverage. For that case, the Texas Supreme Court, in this case sided with a consumer in a dispute over damages caused to the foundation of their home from a water leak.[25]

This problem is not restricted to just this one engineering firm; that firm being one of the biggest, has just been caught more than the others. Also, these are only the cases where there was the will and determination on the part of the insured to hold the insurance company accountable for wrongdoing. We are confident that many more similar acts go undetected or unprosecuted due to the time and cost required to hold an insurance company accountable.

This increased use of biased experts provides insurance companies with a mechanism for issuing denials of legitimate claims, and it has the added benefit of reducing their exposure to bad faith damages. As we discussed in an earlier chapter, bad faith arises when an insurance company intentionally or recklessly delays or denies a claim when their liability is reasonably clear. Thus, when insurance companies retain consultants who prepare biased reports, this gives the insurance company a factual basis for denying the claim. Put another way, the use of such a third-party expert provides the insurance company with a "scapegoat" or an excuse if the claim results in litigation. The insurance company's first defense will be that the damages are as depicted in the engineer's report. Their second defense will be to argue that they simply relied upon the findings of an independent expert and even if those findings were in error, they could not possibly have acted in bad faith!

Under the law, if there is no clear evidence of improper conduct, a dispute over coverage on a claim is said to be "fairly debatable." What this means is that while the insurance company's conclusion may be wrong, the denial of coverage or other claims handling decision does not rise to the level of bad faith conduct. It can be difficult to prove that a consultant did not use reasonable care and generally accepted procedures to investigate the facts before issuing an opinion; and it may be even harder to prove that the insurance company had prior knowledge of this. But in cases such as those referenced above, where there are catastrophic damages to a region, it is easier to compare multiple expert reports to establish a pattern. Unfortunately, most consumers do not have the benefit of multiple reports from a single firm on similar damages to rely upon. In these cases, the claims are often wrongfully denied and consumers are left holding the bag, and paying for losses themselves, losses that they bought insurance to cover.

In our business, we see this every day, and it has become an epidemic in the insurance claim business. In days past, it was only occasionally that we would have a biased expert on a claim file, but today, it is more the rule than the exception. This is not to say that all experts are bad, because nothing could be further from the truth. In fact, we would say that many honestly try to provide a fair and competent opinion on the loss. Regrettably, though, there is an increasing number of such "experts" who will say whatever it takes to make their insurance customers happy.

The fact is that some experts lie and many of them start their lies with their resumes or Curriculum Vitaes (CV's). We routinely find that the CV's of experts exaggerate their training and expertise. We once had an expert present himself as an engineer; however, after an exhaustive investigation, we confirmed that he did not have an engineering degree and he was not qualified to render an opinion on our client's damages. Our qualified engineer's opinion held the day, after this misrepresentation was exposed.

Another recent story involved water damage from a broken water heater in a multi-million dollar home of one our clients. The water heater failed, causing 80 gallons of hot water to leak into the home.

This water caused extensive damages, including damage to the ceramic tile flooring, which is common in water loss claims. Floor tile is installed with a water-based mastic that adheres the tile to the concrete slab. Often, when the floors become saturated by water, the mastic losses it's adherence. The loss of adherence is real damage, as the loose tiles will be subject to increased risk of breakage. It is relatively easy to identify this type of damage by the hollow sound the tile makes when it is tapped with a firm object.

In that case, the insurance company, in an attempt to avoid paying for the replacement of the tile floors, brought in a tile "expert." His CV and his business card alleged that he was from a "ceramic tile institute," which we had never heard of, but it sounded impressive. After some investigation, we made a call to this "institute," where we were told by the person who answered the phone that their main office was not in California, where they listed their office, but in Phoenix, Arizona. We then had an associate call the Phoenix number, where he was told that the main office was in California and that they were just a branch office. As it turned out, these two former tile installers had decided that it was easier to sell their services to insurance companies as tile "experts," rather than doing the backbreaking work of actually installing tile. The whole point of their services seemed to be to write expert reports saying that the tile was not damaged by water, but rather, any damage was due to defective installation. And this was all being done by alleging they were credentialed experts through this fictitious "institute."

Not all experts are employed by insurance companies. Not long ago, we had a claim where the experts were fire investigators for the local fire department. In this loss, the fire investigators made an immediate decision that this fire was intentionally set, and they then engaged in an investigation designed not to find the truth, but to prove their theory. Their approach was proven eventually to not be credible. But, before the truth came out, as a result of this inept fire investigation, our client was arrested for felony arson and placed in jail. When the flawed investigation was finally exposed, the charges were eventually dropped by the county prosecutor's office "in the interest of justice." Regrettably, the insurance company's fire investigators were encouraged to withhold evidence from the prosecutor in an attempt obtain a conviction and to deny coverage for this claim.

It took the retention of real experts, years of litigation and massive costs to prove this customer's innocence in causing the loss. This case eventually received national notoriety through a series of stories on ABC's Nightline News program. Imagine having to endure years of 'litigation hell' to prove your innocence after a fire rips through your home. And imagine that your insurance company is deliberately working against you, subjecting you to the possibility of 27 years in prison for a crime you did not commit, simply to save money on the payment of your claim.

It is a fact that expert reports are not always right. Do not be tricked into thinking that just because your insurance company hired an engineer who wrote a report that identifies another cause of your damages that this opinion is necessarily correct. And just because the "expert" has engineering credentials, this does not mean that he or she is a fair and honest vendor. We have handled dozens of claims where an engineer had authored a report before we were hired that stated there was no damage, and yet more than 98% of those cases ended with our recovery of damages for those clients. In fact, we recently completed a claim on a large apartment complex in Dallas, where the insurer had denied the claim based on an engineer's report stating no hail damage. We settled this claim without litigation for $1.6 million dollars.

The best way you can protect yourself is to ask a lot of questions. Do not allow someone to enter your property without a business card. If your adjuster says he is bringing in an expert, demand that he provide you with the expert's name and CV prior to the visit. You have a right, under the rules of good faith, to know just what credentials the expert has, particularly where that person's expertise is being relied upon by your insurance company to determine the outcome of your claim.

Chapter Nine

Common Estimating Errors and Deceptions

The part of your claim that deals with estimating the costs to repair your home or your commercial building is by far the most difficult part of claims handling to pin down to a specific wrongful practice. Because of the nature of construction estimating, the number of ways that you can be deceived are only limited by the callous intentions of the devious mind. If you do not have extensive knowledge of construction practices and are not familiar with the restoration estimating software that is used to determine the fair value cost to restore your real property to its' pre-loss condition, your chances of obtaining a full fair value claim settlement are highly unlikely. We will attempt here to address some of these improper estimating practices and the more common omissions, but be aware that there are as many ways to cheat as there are cheaters.

One of the more common omissions that we see is the failure to clean surfaces before painting. Whenever a surface is designated to be repainted, the proper method for repainting is to apply the new paint to a clean surface. This step is spelled out on the labels of nearly all paint products manufacturers because their products require a clean surface to adequately cover and adhere to the surface being painted. If your insurer is repainting your walls and ceiling, be sure they have included cleaning into their loss evaluation, or you are being short- changed. This is especially true for exterior painting. In fact, exteriors are even more exposed to dust and dirt than interiors. These surfaces must be cleaned before painting them too. This same process is also required before the application of the smoke sealer coating as well.

Another important area of the loss evaluation to double check is the room and building dimensions. While the Xactimate program now requires the estimator to sketch (draw) the entire building before entering the scope of repair items, there are other versions of this program that do not require the sketch process. In Sketch, if the drawing is accurate, the program will automatically calculate the correct square footages for each scope item. That being said, we still see may mistakes with the area dimension entries and drawing that ware not correctly drawn.

After verification of the dimension entries, the next step is to review the quantities being allowed in the insurer's loss evaluation. There are too many ways to make a mistake to cover in this book, but some of the most common mistakes include roof restorations. This is because some roof operations are entered by the square foot while others are entered by the square (a square is a 10 foot by 10 foot area equal to 100 square feet). Verify that the size of your roof matches the quantities spelled out in their loss evaluation.

Also, another item to double check in the estimate is in their depreciation. As discussed in Chapter 7, insurers commonly depreciate partial repairs. Just because the program nomenclature says replace drywall, this does not mean that this is considered a replacement under an insurance policy. If you are only replacing the bottom two feet of drywall in a room, this is a repair and no depreciation should be applied to this operation. This same procedure holds true for partial roof repairs and for painting of one wall (assuming it can be matched).

Another common practice by insurers is to use the wrong grade (quality) for carpeting, cabinets, lighting fixtures, etc. What Xactimate calls "High Grade" in their program is in reality more of a nice "Builders Grade" product. Ask your adjuster for the printout from Xactimate that provides the operation's description. This "white paper" description spells out the type of quality for this line item in the program.

Assuming you have the correct cabinet grade, the next step is to confirm that your adjuster has included all of the extras that are common to kitchen cabinetry. If your cabinets had handles, this is an add-on item in Xactimate. Did you have glass doors on some of your upper cabinets? This is also an add-on. How about soft close drawers, trash bins, crown moldings? These must all be added on separately, as these are not included in the cabinetry provided by the program. If your cabinetry makes a 90-degree turn, be sure that your adjuster has included the extra charges for this miter cut in his countertop replacement.

If you have suffered a fire loss, be certain that any framing that may have been exposed to smoke and soot is cleaned and sealed properly. We have been in homes that had a fire years earlier and when you walk in the door, you can still smell the odor of fire, even after the home has been restored. This is likely because their insurer and/or their contractor left them with smoke and soot residue in wall cavities and in attic areas.

A new trend in the insurance industry is to take out the cost of many of the items contained in the loss evaluations "General Conditions" area, denoting them as payable "As Incurred." Items such as building permits, engineering costs, architectural costs, temporary toilets, temporary power, temporary fencing, caution tape, commercial or residential supervision are among the more common items that are not included in the insurance company's ACV claim payments.

Just as with contractor's overhead & profit, these scope items are all a part of the actual cash value of the loss. The policy promises to pay you for the actual cash value of loss up front and if you have a replacement cost policy, you can recover the additional holdback monies when repairs are completed. The key to the deceptive nature of this wrongful withholding of your money is based in the policy's promise to pay you the actual cash value of your loss. Like with contractor's overhead & profit, when your home was built, the cost of the home included amounts for building permits, job supervision, architectural plans, engineering plans, a portable toilet for the workers, etc. Therefore, when a loss occurs, a portion of the actual cash value loss would necessarily include these costs. There is no policy requirement we have seen which requires these costs to be incurred before they are owed payment for by your insurer. In fact, under most standard policies, the only losses that must be incurred before they are payable are the depreciation holdback on a replacement cost policy, law & ordinance costs and additional living expenses (ALE) (residential) and loss of business income/extra expenses (commercial). These loss expenses are paid on an "as incurred" basis.

Other than the aforementioned items, your insurer owes you the actual cash value of all other expenses required to restore your property.

You might ask, if they are required to pay these items, why do they not pay them? The answer is simple; it saves them a lot of money. You see, they make up their own rules. The insurance company can say that we do not pay this cost or that cost until it is incurred, but the courts will surely say differently. Unfortunately, most consumers do not want to take these matters to litigation, so the insurance industry gets away with reducing their claim payments through this improper practice.

Also, because most people do not understand their rights under an insurance policy, they do not understand that the insurance company is liable for these payments up front in their actual cash value payment. And like with the past trend to deliberately withhold contractor's overhead & profit, because of the court's ruling in *Campbell*, they can no longer be punished adequately to completely deter this type of wrongful conduct.

If you see the words "As Incurred" on your loss evaluation, demand a written explanation for this position. Also, speak to an attorney or a public adjuster if need be. This is an improper withholding of your money and these types of wrongful practices must be eliminated from the claims adjusting business. Unless consumers hold insurance companies accountable for their written promises that they made when they sold you their policy; this practice is likely to continue. If they don't want to pay these costs in their actual cash value claim payments, they have the power to rewrite their policies to exclude these costs, rather than misinterpreting this coverage. As mentioned in the previous chapter, that is exactly what Farmer's did in their insurance policy endorsement 7122, with several of these construction costs. Depending upon the jurisdiction where you are located, these types of policy provisions might actually be legal.

Chapter Ten

Coinsurance Deceptions and Improper Applications of Deductibles

Coinsurance requirements are common in insurance policies, yet few people outside of the insurance business know what they are and how they work. Coinsurance is the joint assumption of risk by two or more parties. In a typical property insurance policy, it is usually the risk assumed by the insurance company and that assumed by the consumer. The purpose of this policy provision is to encourage consumers to accurately report the values of property so that they do not under-insurance their property. You might ask, why would anyone deliberately under-insure their property. The answer is simple. The vast majority of losses are only partial losses, so the chance of needing the policy extent of policy coverage is rare. So a thrifty consumer can save money in the form of the premiums paid for their policy by insuring their property for less than its full value.

In order to deter this type of under-insurance, many policies have a coinsurance requirement. The most common coinsurance requirement is 80%, which means that the consumer must insure his property for at least 80% of its full replacement cost value. If a loss occurs and the insurance company discovers that the coinsurance requirement has not been met, they can assess a coinsurance penalty against the consumer to recover a portion of the loss. This forces the policyholder to participate in the loss up to the required percentage.

To better explain this, let's use an example. Bob has a commercial building with a current replacement value of $150,000 that he has insured for $100,000. The policy he purchased has an 80% coinsurance requirement. Bob has a fire loss that does $50,000 in damage to his building. The insurance adjuster does a calculation of the replacement cost of his building as it was at the time of loss and determines that the replacement cost of his building was $150,000. Assuming that he had a $500 policy deductible, Bob's claim payable would be calculated as follows:

Loss payable =
$\underline{\text{Coverage purchased}}$ × Loss − Deductible
(Property value × coinsurance)
Hence, Bob's claim would be paid as follows:
$\underline{\$100,000}$ or $\underline{\$100,000}$ = .8333 × $50,000
($150,000*80%) $120,000
= $41, 665 − $500 = $41,165 claim payable

Consequently, Bob must participate in this loss not only with his deductible, but because he under-insured his property, he only receives a prorated portion of his loss. This decision cost Bob an additional $8,335 plus his deductible. Had Bob insured his property properly, his only cost would have been the policy deductible.

But, what if Bob did not really under-insure his property? What if the methods used by his adjuster do not accurately calculate the real replacement cost of his building?

Other questions also arise from this, such as: What is Bob's expertise in determining the value of his building? Did Bob rely upon his agent to set the policy limits? What is his agent's responsibility for setting the policy limits of coverage? And what responsibility does the insurance company's policy Underwriter have in this determination of the appropriate levels of coverage Bob needs to fully insure his building? Did the insurance company or the agent ever inform Bob that he was under-insuring his building before the loss?

This is a complex issue that requires a great deal of skill and investigation into how the policy coverage limits were set and who was responsible for this determination. Also, the laws vary from state to state on whether or not an agent can be held liable for an error in the placement of coverage.

So why bring this issue up here? The reason is that we are seeing an increase in the numbers of claims that are being scrutinized by insurers for meeting the policy's coinsurance requirements and we are seeing egregious miscalculations of what is to be included in insurance company's calculation of the replacement cost valuation. Suffice it to say that it is easy for an adjuster to exaggerate the full replacement cost of a building if he is so motivated. And we believe that the insurance company's underwriter has some responsibility to the policyholder to inform him if he is selecting a policy limit that does not meet the coinsurance requirements. We often refer to the belated application of coinsurance to a loss as "post-loss underwriting."

It is easy to see how an insurer could be motivated to exaggerate the coinsurance penalty so as to save money in claims payments. And as you remember from the first couple of chapters, every dollar saved in claim payments is another dollar of net income for the insurance company.

Another very common improper claims practice is with the application of the policy deductible. This issue has been the subject of several articles over the years, yet we continue to see the same improper applications of deductibles time after time. The issue is with the absorption of the deductible by the excess losses.

We are taught in our formal insurance industry training to first apply the policy deductible to the total loss and then to apply any limitations of coverage as set forth in the policy. However, we often see adjusters applying the policy deductible to the loss payable portion of the claim, rather than the total loss. This difference can be best explained through an example.

Let's assume that Rick has a homeowner's policy which includes coverage for theft and has a policy deductible of $100.00. While Rick was on vacation, a burglar broken into Ricks home and stole his TV which had a replace value of $500, his camera valued at $400 and $350 in cash that Rick had in his nightstand. Rick's policy is a standard ISO form HO-3 which has a limitation of coverage for cash of $200.

Rick's total loss from this theft event is as follows:

TV $500
Camera $400 Cash $350
Total Loss $1,250
Rick's loss payable from this theft would be as follows: TV $500
Camera $400
Cash ($350- special limit) $200
Total Loss $1,100

Rick's adjuster would not allowed to apply the $100 policy deductible to the loss payable because the special limit of coverage for theft of cash left Rick with an uncovered loss of $150 and as such, Rick has already participated in the loss through his excess loss.

We often see adjusters fail to properly absorb a policy deductible as they should, without us first bringing it to their attention. In fact, we know of insurance companies that deliberately instruct their adjusters to not properly apply policy deductibles to claims, as we observed first-hand after Hurricane Floyd.

The wrongful practice in applying deductibles was also common following the Northridge earthquake and led to expensive litigation for some insurers who were misapplying the policy deductibles for earthquake losses. Certain insurers got sued because they calculated the 10% earthquake deductible on the total amount of coverage written, rather than as 10% of the amount of the claim.

One such instance involved a large California HOA that had an $85 million dollar policy, where the insurance company was applying an $8.5 million dollar deductible to their $10.5 million dollar loss. When the HOA board asked Victor and I if we could help them, Victor and I just looked at each other and smiled and assured them that we could indeed help. The reason for our smile was that we both knew we could recover a quick $6 million dollars in unpaid claim benefits just by raising this misapplication of the deductible to the insurer. This issue turned into a major class action lawsuit in California following the Northridge earthquake.

There is no reason that a consumer under an insurance policy should have to retain help to obtain the benefits that they paid for, yet day after day, the need for professional representation becomes ever more apparent. The claims game is rigged and it more often than not requires someone who knows the rules and knows how to play the game as well or better than the insurance company.

Chapter Eleven

Matching and Cosmetic Losses

One of the most important claim issues, and one that has a significant impact on homeowners is the issue of "matching." What happens when the lower kitchen cabinets are damaged by a water line break, but replacement cabinets to match the upper cabinets are no longer available? What if the roof is damaged by a windstorm and matching roof shingles are no longer available? What is the insurance company's responsibility under the policy?

The answer to this question lies more on where you live than with what the policy says. This is an issue that has been litigated many times, and because the matter involves insurance, which must be litigated on a state-by-state basis, the answer to this question is different depending upon which court makes the ruling. Some courts vigorously adhere to the basic principles of indemnity, holding that repair of damages must result in an aesthetically pleasing result. Or in laymen's terms, the repairs must match the existing building components in materials, colors and finishes.

Other courts have been more restrictive in their interpretation of the policy's promise of coverage, ruling that the policy is only intended to replace the portions of the building that actually suffered damages from a covered peril. This reasoning ignores the traditional application of coverage by insurance companies and it mistakenly buys in to the insurance companies' misreading of their own policies. In these cases, the courts have ruled that the insurance policy does not require the insurer to replace areas that were not damaged. Regrettably, this leaves the consumer with either a mismatched area of their building or a huge out of pocket cost to make an aesthetically proper repair.

In the mid-1990's, when this issue first surfaced, we wrote to the well- respected insurance treatise, FC&S Bulletins, which is a subsidiary of the Insurance Services Office who is the author of the ISO insurance policies used by most insurance companies. The FC&S Bulletins is a publication that discusses how the language of the policies that they write is intended to be interpreted. An additional feature of the FC&S Bulletins is a question and answer (Q&A) section that is published periodically, where claims adjusters can write in presenting a specific set of facts on one of their claims and the editors of the FC&S Bulletins provide a detailed explanation of how the policy language should respond to these situations. It is very informative and interesting to read some of the questions and answers in this publication.

One such question which we presented asked about the new positions (at that time) being taken by insurance companies, stating that their policies do not owe to match. The editors of the FC&S provided a well- reasoned answer to this question. At that time, insurance companies were taking the position that if the upper cabinets were not damaged, they did not owe to replace them, even though the new lower cabinets would not match the existing upper cabinets. Similar arguments were being made as to matching many other building components, such as roof shingles or exterior siding.

The insurance companies devised a creative argument in an attempt to restrict coverage by arguing that the policy states that they will repair or replace "that part of the building" that is damaged. In their view "that part of a building" meant each individual shingle or individual piece of siding, rather than the more logical interpretation that "a shingle may be part of a building, but is more properly a part of a roof." Similarly, a strip of siding is a part of a wall. And it is the walls and the roof that become 'parts' of the building.

The editors of the FC&S Bulletins shocked the insurance world with their resounding affirmation that "yes" indeed the insurance policy does in fact owe the insured for a matching repair. They supported their opinion citing the basic tenets of insurance, the "principle of indemnity" and the insured's "reasonable expectations." They said, "The insured is told that he will be made whole and restored to a pre- loss condition; based on this promise, he reasonably expects this will be done in the event of a loss. He expects to be fully indemnified."

It has been many years since this FC&S editor's opinion was first issued. Since this time, the FC&S Bulletins has hedged their position somewhat, acknowledging that the issue of matching has been adjudicated in courtrooms across the country with differing results. However, even today, the editor's in the on-line version of FC&S Bulletins maintains that in their opinion, the insurance policy should owe for matching repairs.

The results of the various court decisions give us different rules for different jurisdictions. So the question of whether your insurance policy covers matching repairs, may be more a function of where you live than what your policy says.

Another resource to check is your state's Unfair Claims Practices statues for guidance. In the National Association of Insurance Commissioner's model Unfair Claims Practices act, they have included language that requires matching of building components and finishes. Unfortunately, the individual states legislatures make the determination as to what provisions are to be included in their final state law and several states have not fully adopted the NAIC's model act in full leaving the matching provisions out of the required claims handling conduct.

While the majority have found that the insurance company owes for matching repairs in the event of a covered loss, there have been some decisions that confound the logical mind. One such case is that of the 2008 Texas Court of Appeals ruling in the *All Saints Catholic Church*[26] matter. In this ridiculous ruling, the court took the position that the insurance company only owed for the cost of replacing the individual roof tiles that suffered hail damage, even though these roof tiles were no longer available and in spite of the fact presented that to remove the damaged tiles would damage many more tiles. The court ignored the fact that replacement tiles could not be installed without damaging the existing tiles and they ignored the fact that the new tiles would not match the existing tiles in their ruling. According to this court, it was acceptable that the church, after suffering a covered loss would have to pay out of pocket for a substantial portion of the repairs to their roof, even though they had a properly functioning roof prior to this hailstorm.

Notwithstanding this court decision, in a very recent litigation over matching, the Minnesota Supreme Court in *Cedar Bluff* [27] has weighed in, in favor of coverage for matching repairs to the Associations exterior siding when it was shown that the existing siding was no longer available, and the new siding did not match the existing siding. In their ruling, the court stated that "…the plain meaning of the phrase 'comparable material and quality' is material that is *suitable* for matching.…Therefore, in accordance with the plain meaning of the policy language, we construe the phrase 'comparable material and quality' to mean a reasonable color match between new and existing siding when replacing damaged siding."

The court went on to address American Family's argument that the policy did not require them to replace siding that was not damaged. As we discussed above, the insurance company's argument is based upon the idea that the policy only owes to repair the damaged siding. This court analyzed American Family's argument by looking into the policy's promise of coverage for "direct physical loss of or damage" and American Family's own definition of the term "physical damage" meaning a distinct, demonstrable, and physical alteration." In this regard, the court rejected the piece-by-piece approach but instead looked at the siding as a whole as they ruled that "Because of the color mismatch resulting from the inability to replace the hail-damaged siding panels with siding of 'comparable material and quality' the covered property – Cedar Bluff's 'buildings' – has sustained a 'distinct, demonstrable, and physical alteration.' Thus, we conclude that the covered property sustained a covered loss."

This court decision and many similar decisions have forced the insurance companies to resort to a new tactic. Rather than taking on the issue of matching directly, they have devised a new tactic.

You see the insurance industry never seems to exhaust their list of tricks to avoid coverage for losses. Their creative use of semantics to make arguments against coverage seems endless.

Remember that about twenty years ago, the Insurance Industry came to the conclusion that they did not have to pay contractor's overhead & profit costs until these costs were "incurred," despite the fact that their policies make no mention of the word "incurred" as a requirement of indemnification. As this issue became the subject of multiple lawsuits across the country, insurance companies eventually found it to be unprofitable to continue this practice. Unfortunately, the manner in which insurance is regulated in the United States forces consumers to fight the same battles in each state. So while they started to pay contractor overhead & profit costs on claim payments in those jurisdictions where they had lost, they continued to withhold these costs in the states that had not yet ruled on the contractor overhead & profit issue.

The latest trend is in response to the multitude of hail damage claims from Texas to Arizona. It is not that there are really more hailstorms, but there are more roofing contractors who have discovered that they can make a very good living (chasing) following these storm events.

The insurance industry seems to be engaged in a concerted effort to encourage their favorite engineers and consultants to include qualifying language in their expert reports to be later used as the basis to deny coverage. The reason we say concerted effort is because it seems unlikely that all of a sudden we would start seeing the same references in reports from different engineering firms and on behalf of different insurance companies, all appearing at or about the same time period, if not for a concerted effort by the insurance industry to steer firms in this direction. Either that or these engineering firms all woke up one day and decided independently to insert similar qualifying language into their description of damages in their expert reports. You be the judge.

The most recent trend is for these favored consultants/experts to identify damages in terms of "functional damages vs. cosmetic damages." Of course, the implication here and the application of this argument is that "cosmetic damages" are not real damage and are not to be afforded coverage under the insurance policy. In looking to the standard language of the ISO form HO-3 policy, the "HO 003 10 00" policy sets forth coverage as follows: "We insure against risk of direct loss to property described in Coverages A and B." The policy then goes into a laundry list of losses that are excluded from coverage under this policy, none of which containing any discussion of either cosmetic or functional damages.

Even more excluded losses can be found in the policy's Exclusions provision, things like Law and Ordinance, Earth Movement, Nuclear Hazard, Intentional Loss, etc. but still nothing at all about cosmetic or functional damages.

In the commercial policy, the ISO form CP 10 30 Causes of Loss - Special Form sets forth coverage as follows:

"A. Covered Causes Of Loss
When Special is shown in the Declarations, Covered Causes of Loss means Risks Of Direct Physical Loss unless the loss is:

1. Excluded in Section B., Exclusions; or
2. Limited in Section C., Limitations; that follow."

Again, there is no reference at all to cosmetic or functional damages either in the insuring agreement language or in the Exclusions provisions. So where then is this coming from? While we are not industry insiders, we suspect that this is being orchestrated by the insurance industry's Property Loss Research Bureau (PLRB), which is an association of insurance companies dedicated to the advancement of insurance company coverage issues. Their defense attorney's apparently get together to brainstorm insurance defense procedures and it is self-evident that they routinely find inventive ways to bolster insurer's profits through creative new arguments to limit or deny coverage for damages. There can be no other explanation for multiple different insurance companies and different engineering firms all mysteriously using the same unique terminology at about the same time. Of course, maybe it is just a coincidence.

The fact remains that no standard form insurance policy makes a distinction between "cosmetic vs. functional" damages or sets forth exclusions for such. Yet, over the last four or five years, we have had multiple insurers attempt to make this argument on our client's claims. In a recent case that we submitted to be resolved through the policy's appraisal provision, our appraiser called us and said that the other appraiser is arguing that some of the damages to the property are purely cosmetic and not functional damages. We suggested that at their next meeting, he back into the other appraiser's car fender and then tell him that he is very sorry, but that the damage is only cosmetic and not functional damage. It would be interesting to see his reaction. We have no doubt that he will not be OK with that!

Imagine if your auto insurer was to rely upon such a distinction? There would be millions of cars driving around with dented fenders and bumpers. Some might look like they have been in a demolition derby. If a hailstorm damages your car, is that cosmetic or functional damages? Is it covered? Of course, it is cosmetic and yes, it is covered if you purchased a comprehensive insurance auto policy. They would have a really hard time selling automobile insurance policies if they attempted to exclude cosmetic damages from coverage, as that is one major motivator to buying auto insurance in the first place; to protect your investment in your car from accident damages.

Having insurance coverage is also a requirement of the bank that loans you the money to buy your car, so that it is protected by insurance in the case of damage. This is likewise the point of purchasing homeowner's insurance protection; to protect your investment in "real" property from damages, be it cosmetic or functional.

Do not allow yourself to be tricked into this insurance trap. This language is deliberately designed to underpay or deny legitimate claims. There is no distinction in most policies between cosmetic and functional damages. Damage is damage, period; and the policy's promise is for coverage to repair or replace the damaged building component, just the same as it does for your car and in most states the promise of coverage includes matching repairs.

Be careful though because some insurers are inserting endorsements that limit coverage for the cost of repairs to match or provide new language for functional damages. You must be cognizant of the jurisdiction in which your property is located, as the controlling case law varies significantly from one state to the next, as do the state laws that regulate insurance. To get a definitive answer, start by reviewing the policy coverages and endorsements, check the state insurance statutes and then find an attorney who knows applicable case law in your jurisdiction.

Chapter Twelve

Emerging Issues/Final Thoughts

Insurance companies are expert in accessing and transferring risks. From the ancient Chinese and <u>Babylonian</u> traders in the 3rd and 2nd

millennia BC to the 1st millennium BC, the inhabitants of Rhodes who organized groups of merchants to pay to insure their goods being shipped together[28], the importance of insurance to a civilized society was clear as was the recognition that the spreading of the risk among the many at a small price could protect the few from certain financial disaster. Hence was the birth of today's insurance model, which is built upon the concept of the law of large numbers. Actuaries analyze the financial consequences of risk through mathematics, statistics and financial theory to predict the likely cost and probability of a loss event. They have become so proficient that they can predict with near certainty the number of fire losses that any major city will have this year.

Armed with this information, insurance companies can offer insurance products that provide financial security to consumers while assuring a fair profit for the insurance company. In recent years we have seen several major catastrophic loss events, yet, in the last 100 years, the property casualty insurance market has only shown a loss in one year. That is just one year in a hundred! Their modeling is obviously very good in predicting loss events. Likewise, insurance companies have become very good at avoiding the most likely and costly loss events by transferring these risks to government. This transfer of risk has resulted in the National Flood Insurance Program for flood damage, along our southeastern coastline we have the Citizens Property Insurance Corporation for hurricane and wind damage insurance coverage and in California there is earthquake coverage, via the California Earthquake Authority or California Fair Plan and Texas has a windstorm and hail coverage program under their TWIA Texas Wind Insurance Association. While in most instances, insurance companies are required to participate in these programs, the major responsibility for the excess risk of loss for these programs falls upon the federal and/or state governments and ultimately the taxpayers.

Similar actions in the transfer of risk are being seen in the middle of the country with respect to inland wind and hail losses. Insurance companies are changing their policies to include large wind and hail deductibles that are separate and distinct from the standard policy deductible. Other changes of late include policy Exclusions for cosmetic damages and ACV (Actual Cash Value) Roof Endorsements which amend the policy to only pay for the actual cash value of the roof in the event of a covered loss, if the roof is more than 10 years old, even if you have a replacement cost policy on the property. In many cases, our clients were surprised to find these provisions in their policies, so it is safe to say that in many cases the consumers are not being adequately notified of these significant changes to their insurance coverage.

Also, we are seeing insurance companies adding provisions that provide coverage for repairs with "common construction and similar materials." The ISO has authored policy coverage forms for insurance companies to amend the coverage provided to Functional Replacement Cost coverage in their ISO HO 05 30 05 11 and HO 05 31 11 policy forms. These changes in insurance coverage have one common element; they pay less in the event of a covered loss.

Recently, one of America's major insurance companies has begun a practice in preparing their loss evaluations that we believe will ultimately end up in litigation. The computer software known as Xactimate is offered to its' users with more than one pricelist database. They offer a "restoration" pricelist and they offer a "new construction" pricelist. With the flip of a switch, the adjuster can switch between these pricelists allegedly to account for the project being evaluated. The restoration pricelist is developed to account for the costs of restoring or repairing damages an existing building. The "new construction" pricelist was developed to estimate the construction costs for a new building. The differences in costs vary by the type of work that is being estimated, but the general rule is that the "new construction" pricelist will yield a significantly lower cost of construction than the "restoration" pricelist will.

The reason for this is that when engaging in restoration work, the contractor must work around existing building components. He must protect the existing finishes and fixtures from being damaged as he goes about the restoration work. During construction of a new building, the trades are scheduled to complete their portion of the work in a sequence that makes many of these precautions that a restoration contractor might take unnecessary.

For instance, when considering interior painting of a building, in new construction, the interior painting is most often done before there are any floor covering, lighting fixtures and furnishings to protect from overspray paint damages. As such, the painting of a new home or building would be less expensive to complete, because the time required to do the work is reduced.

Similarly, when engaging in "new construction" the various subcontractors do not have to worry about working around existing landscaping, fences or sideways. A roofing contractor can drive a forklift right up to the building to deliver the roof shingles for installation. Driving a forklift up to an existing structure would likely cause damages to lawns, sprinkler systems, shrubbery, etc., making it necessary to hand-carry the materials onto the roof. The "new construction pricelist takes into consideration the cost savings of building a new building from the ground up.

The latest practice by one insurer is to use the "new construction" pricelist on the partial repair (restoration) of a home that has been fire damaged. Despite repeated attempts to correct this wrongful claim practice, this insurer has refused to budge. Their adjuster, whom we have known for years just shrugs his shoulders and says that this is being dictated by their corporate office and he has no choice except to follow instructions. The net result on one recent claim is an underpayment of nearly $10,000, when compared to the same project evaluated with the restoration pricelist. Obviously, underpaying claims in this manner will reduce this insurance company's cost of claims and like with their wrongful practices of withholding contractor's overhead & profit, they know eventually they will get caught, get sued and have to pay out some money over this practice. But the money they save in the meantime, still makes this sort of conduct profitable. Many thanks again can go to the United States Supreme Court for their errant wisdom in the *Campbell* ruling. When insurance companies cannot get what they want through their lobbying efforts of government agencies and politicians to change the laws, they just ignore the laws until they are sued enough times that it makes these wrongful practices, impractical to continue. Even today, we still find insurance companies failing to pay contractor's overhead & profit on claims.

Judging by all of these changes, one would think that there is some huge problem with insurance companies losing money, yet as we mentioned above, they have only lost money once in the last 100 years. What then is the driving force for all of these changes? The answer is obvious; profits, profits, and more profits. While we all want and need our insurance providers to be profitable for the overall good of society, the increases in revenues generated in the property and casualty insurance market are unprecedented in comparison to any other historical period of time. Insurance companies are no longer satisfied to just make a fair profit, they now seek to maximize their profits and, as such, are making more money now than ever before.

In fact, according to a recent report by Property Casualty Insurers Association of America, "Private U.S. property/casualty insurers' net income after taxes grew to $63.8 billion in 2013 from $35.1 billion in 2012....

Insurers' overall results for 2013 also benefited from a $4.6 billion increase in net investment gains — the sum of net investment income and realized capital gains (or losses) on investments — which rose to $58.8 billion in 2013 from $54.2 billion in 2012.

The $66.3 billion increase in policyholders' surplus to a record-high $653.3 billion at year-end 2013 is a testament to the strength and safety of insurers' commitment to policyholders. Insurers are strong, well-capitalized, and well prepared to pay future claims," said Robert Gordon, PCI's senior vice president for policy development and research[29]."

Clearly, the property casualty industry is alive and well in America and it is not by accident. Insurance companies' ability to transfer the higher risk loss events to government agencies and the changes instituted in claims handling since the recommendations of McKinsey and Accenture have led to a drastic increase in profitability. Whether it is the government, of which we are all taxpayers, or us as individuals, we are all bearing the increased cost of property insurance and this trend is not likely to change for the better any time soon.

Insurance companies with their billions of dollars in profits have significant influence over politicians, so it is unlikely that any relief will come from government. And, because most state departments of insurance are filled with people who received their industry training while working for insurance companies, it can be difficult to find true consumer advocates there. It is important to note; however, that we have seen immense progress in the last few years within some of these state regulatory agencies. While many in these agencies really try to do good work to protect the public, budget restraints and the influence of the insurance industry often serve to work against the publics' interests. One common change we have noticed within these state departments of insurance is that they are no longer preapproving policy forms, but instead are taking the file and use approach. They only look into the actual changed policy if a complaint is filed. As such, consumers can expect to continuously pay more and get less in the foreseeable future.

Notwithstanding the fact that the deck is significantly stacked against them, insurance consumers can still effectively get the coverage that they have paid for in the event of a loss, provided they enter the process with an understanding of just how the game is played. Winning in the game of claim negotiations takes training and skills that most claimants do not possess, but the ability to identify wrongful claim settlement practices can help significantly to putting you on the road to a fair recovery. Some of the most common improper claim practices have been examined in these pages, not to make the reader a claim adjuster, but to help consumers identify unfair treatment when they see it. Knowing that you are not being treated fairly by your adjuster is the first critical step to recovering the fair value of your claim.

Whether you choose to do it yourself or you obtain assistance from an attorney or a public adjuster, an understanding of **The Claims Game** and how it is played can provide you a path to a full recovery of your loss. Understanding The Claims Game can help you to avoid the financial consequences that can result from the insurance company's **Broken Promises.**

APPENDIX I

Claim Basics 101

There is no way the lessons in this book can turn you into a claims adjuster and truly place you on equal footing with the insurance company; however, by following these simple steps you may be able to prevent your claim from becoming the one that ends up in years of litigation. At the very least, heeding this advice will put you in a much better position for a fair claim settlement. If you are not willing to put in the effort to perform these simple steps, then you might seriously consider retaining professional representation.

The steps that we recommend below are the same steps that our professional adjusters follow and all public adjusters should follow. Unfortunately, human beings have a tendency to be lazy, which often leads to overlooking good claims handling practices. We constantly are reminding our adjusters of the importance of documenting the claim files, to keep an accurate record of everything that happens on the claim, until the final check is received.

1. Do Not Sign a Direct Pay Authorization

As mentioned in the previous chapter, the first step in a loss recovery is often to initiate emergency services to prevent further damages to the property. You will be told that this is your duty under the policy to protect the property and this is correct. Most often, the restoration contractor sent out by the insurance company and even those who arrive at your door just after the loss happens will present you with what they describe as simply a work authorization form. But, most often, these forms contain a direct payment authorization, which allows them to present their bills to the insurance company and the insurance company is being told by your signature on their authorization that it is OK for them to pay the contractor directly. Many consumers are never even told how much the emergency services bills are before they are paid. This is a really bad idea. If you are unhappy with their work, or if they do other damages to your property, you have no recourse with them, because they already have all of their money, "your money." If they will not delete the direct payment authorization from their contract, find another contractor who will.

2. Obtain a certified copy of the policy

The first place to start in the processing of a claim is to know what is covered under the policy of insurance that was in place at the time of the loss. It is for this reason that our first request is for production of a certified copy of the insurance policy. Doing this will ensure that you are working from the correct policy for this loss. Policies change from year to year, so do not rely upon an old copy or even a new copy you may have in your insurance file. These policies may differ substantially from the policy in effect at the time of the current loss event.

Place your request to your insurer in writing and keep a copy for your file. If they do not respond in a timely manner, contact your state Department of Insurance for assistance. Helping consumers get a copy of their insurance policy is one of the areas that these agencies really excel in, so don't be afraid to seek their assistance. The insurance company is required to provide you this document.

Read the policy to get a better understanding of the coverage provided and the terms of payment. This is not an easy task, which is why few people actually read their policies. If you are not willing to take the time to read your policy, you should seriously consider hiring professional representation. Unfortunately, even if you do read your policy it is quite possible that you may not really understand it and the coverages it provides. This is because it is common for insurance policies to provide coverage in one section, then take it away or limit it in another section. In some of the more complex commercial policies, it is possible that the policy provides coverage, takes it away, then gives it back, but limits it in another section. It can be difficult to understand exactly what the terms of your coverage, but it is not impossible with some effort.

3. Obtain a copy of the Unfair Claims Practices Act

Go to the internet and download a copy of your state's "Unfair Claims Practices." These can be found in your state insurance statutes and they are easy to read and to understand. They give you more or less the play book that the insurance company is required to follow. It provides information on how long the adjuster has to investigate your claim, how long he has to respond to your written communications and how long they have to issue payment of your claim. Knowing these regulations can be very helpful in keeping your claim moving to conclusion.

4. Keep a claim log

From day one, get a notebook and enter every activity that happens on your claim. Record every phone call, every meeting, and every claim activity and make good notes as to exactly what was discussed and agreed upon. Even if you did not start a claim log on day one of your claim, start one right now and go back in your mind and write down everything that you can remember. Your memory will not be any better two years from now when you are in court than it is today, so do not delay in doing this. And if your wife or husband or other relatives witnessed any of these meetings, have them write their own account of the meetings. Do not work together! Work separately because each person is likely to remember things the other did not, so by working separately and then combining these notes, you will have a better history of the claim.

While it may seem unlikely that your claim will ever go to litigation, if your claim does go badly, this logbook will be an invaluable record of the claim events and will significantly help your case against the insurance company. As we tell our adjusters in our training seminars, "we always approach a new claim by hoping for the best, but preparing for the worst."

We cannot tell you the numbers of times we hear new clients tell us that they made agreements with their adjuster, and then their claim was reassigned to a new adjuster who refuses to acknowledge or honor those agreements.

We recently had a client who reached an agreement with her adjuster for repair of damages to her pool equipment caused by the firefighting activities. She did not document this agreement before her claim was reassigned to another adjuster. The new adjuster refused to pay for these repairs and when confronted with the fact that the other adjuster agreed to these costs, he said that in his opinion the damages were not caused by the fire department and the previous adjuster made no notes in this matter. Without any notation of the prior agreement, it was back to square one in getting the new adjuster's agreement to pay for these repairs. A simple email to the prior adjuster confirming this agreement is all it would have taken to preserve the record of this agreement.

5. Confirm all communications in writing

It is critical that you document in writing every meeting and telephone call with the insurance company and with any of their contractors. These do not have to be full blown legal letters, just a simple confirmation of a telephone call and what was discussed and agreed upon during the call or confirmation of agreements made at a personal meeting. Ask the adjuster to provide a written explanation if you have misstated any of the agreements. Documenting the claims process is also important to preventing unreasonable delays in the processing of your claim. A simple letter confirming that the adjuster is working on his estimate and will have it done by Friday can be very effective in holding him accountable and moving your claim to a timely settlement.

When deciding what media to use, in dealing with insurance companies, a written letter is far more effective than an email. Today, even though email provides a written record of events, because it is so common in our everyday lives, people tend to view an email just as though it were a telephone conversation. Hence, emails will work but they are not as effective as written and mailed letters.

Also, many insurers have specific requirements of adjusters that require them to give a written response to letters received by the insurance company. From our experience, adjusters hate having to write letters, so a persistent written campaign can help push the timely settlement of your claim.

Be very careful what you put in a letter. Do not let your emotions get the best of you and do not send something that might later be embarrassing in front of a jury. If you are too emotional, write it down and let it sit overnight before you send it, so that have time to think about what you have said. Over the years we have seen some shocking things said in writing by our clients to their adjuster and vice versa; like one who asked his adjuster if he beat his dog before or after his morning coffee. These comments, while they might feel good at the moment are like winning a battle, when the objective is not to win a battle but to win the war.

Keeping and accurate record of each and every event in your claim is of the utmost importance to getting a fair claim settlement. This written communication to the adjuster places him on notice that you are recording everything he or she does on your claim. In our experience, a well-documented claim is one that usually gets paid faster and more fully.

6. Photograph everything

As soon as possible, make a photographic record of all building damages and of all personal property, damaged and undamaged. If possible, photograph personal property items separately, even if there is only a trace of the damaged item because insurance companies are constantly questioning the existence of property, even property they have already seen in their initial inspection. It is not uncommon for adjusters to get amnesia after they complete their initial loss inspection, and the damaged property is already thrown away. Even after we reached an agreement with the adjuster on Bill and Ruth's claim in chapter one, six months later the insurance adjuster was replaced by a new adjuster and she continues to question the quantity of damaged items even when provided photographic evidence.

Also, thieves have a way of knowing when a property has had a loss and they know the property is unlikely to be occupied. Even the theft of items that are a total loss can be problematic when trying to obtain payment for them from your insurance company. While the insurer still owes you for the items, it is much harder to prove that you had them and much more difficult to prove their value. Take tons of pictures!

With today's digital media, it costs nothing to take a lot so pictures to save them as a record of your belongings.

We once had an insurance company questioning our client's claim submission, believing that they were claiming items that they did not have. As you can imagine, after a total loss fire there usually is very little evidence left. In this instance, the insurance company was questioning the existence of an exercise bike. We honestly could not remember the bike and were perplexed by how we were going to prove that our client had one. Then in reviewing some of our photos taken the day of our first inspection of the building, there in the rubble was the frame and wheel from the exercise bike in question. We got lucky that this was in the picture, as it was not what we were taking a picture of, but submitting this photo to the insurer got our client's paid for the lost exercise bike.

While you are at it, get a video camera and take a good video of the property and all of the damaged contents. Video footage coupled with photographs can be very helpful in documenting your loss.

7. Do not throw away anything until you have the check in your hand

Even if you have an agreement with the insurance company that certain items are a total loss and they have authorized you to throw them away, wait until you get their check, do not be suckered into thinking that you have a firm agreement with them. Hold on to all property until you have a written agreement from the insurer as to the value of these items and then hold them until payment is received.

Just in case a new claim handler takes over your claim, you must protect yourself. What if you end up having to go to appraisal to determine the fair value of your loss? How will the appraisers know the true value of your items without being able to see them? Hold all property regardless of its condition until payment is received.

8. Do not start building repairs until you have a complete agreement in place

Even though you may have a verbal agreement, we do not recommend starting repairs until you have their position in writing and know for certain exactly what your insurance company is willing to pay you for your loss. If you alter the loss scene and later must demand appraisal to set the value of your loss, it can be much harder in some instances for the appraisers to really see your building as it was and this can have a serious impact on the amount of your recovery.

What happens if you tear down a damaged wall and then the insurance company takes the position that that wall was not damaged by the loss and they refuse to pay for it? How can you prove that the wall was damaged in the loss if it is already gone? We have had consumers bring hail damage claims to us that are in dispute, where they have already done a new coating over the damages. How can we prove it was damaged after the evidence has been destroyed?

Do not start any work until a complete settlement agreement has been reached. It is not in your best interest to change the loss scene until a fair resolution has been reached. Insurer often pressure customers to start demolition before the claim settlement has been finalized. They sometime suggest that it is your duty under the policy to mitigate your loss. While it is true that the policyholder does have a duty to mitigate e their loss, this duty does not mean that you must start repairs before you know how much money you will have to complete the restoration. If your adjuster tells you this, tell him that you cannot contract for the repairs until you know how much money the insurance company is going to pay you to complete the repairs. Starting the work before you have a final agreement with the insurance company only benefits the insurance company.

We have had clients that ignored our warnings and moved forward with repairs, only to find out that the insurance company was not in agreement with the scope of repairs to their building. How can you prove that replacing your roof was the only logical means to restoring your roof, rather than just some partial repair, once the roof has been replaced?

Also, who will end up making up the difference, if your contractor starts making repairs that the insurance company eventually refuses to pay for? That's right; it may come out of your pocket. As much as you may be in a hurry to get your property repaired as quickly as possible, you must be patient until your have their written agreement and their check.

9. Obtaining the full policy benefits for replacement of building & personal property

Insurance policies differ somewhat on the replacement cost benefits offered and what is required to obtain them, but under most standard form replacement cost insurance policies, the insurance company does not have to pay you the full replacement cost value of your claim until you actually make the repairs or replacements.

Before getting into the details on how these policy requirements work, let us start by explaining some of the terminology that is used in insurance. The term replacement cost value or RCV means just that; it is the current replacement cost of the item that is being replaced. The term actual cash value or ACV is, in most jurisdictions the replacement cost value of the item minus an amount called depreciation to account for the age or wear and tear, etc. of the item. What is left is the actual cash value of that item. Most policies written today only require the insurance company to pay you the actual cash value of your loss until repairs are completed.

Therefore, it is critical that you do not assume that simply completing repairs or replacements will result in another check for the full amount of the depreciation the insurer is holding, which is usually referred to a depreciation holdback. Insurance companies word these policies for their own benefit, not for yours. If they can sell you the illusion of replacement cost coverage and never have to pay up fully, then they win. Do you remember McKinsey's reference to insurance being a zero sum game?

There are ways to recover your full replacement cost value, if you know how to play their game and if you are very diligent in tracking the replacement of items. The following examples will help to understand how these Loss Payment provisions work and enable you to more fully recover the replacement value of your loss.

Personal Property Example

Let's assume that you lost a 55-inch TV in a fire. The insurance company has agreed that the replacement cost of this TV is $800.00, but because it was 4 years old, they have taken off 40% for depreciation or $320.00 from your claim payment leaving you with $480.00 to buy a new TV. So you go down to Walmart and find that they have 55 inch TV's on sale for $675.00. You are thrilled by your luck in finding this item on sale, so you buy it expecting to submit the receipt get your $320.00 check.

Not so fast; most of these policies are worded in a manner that you get the $800.00 only if you actually spend $800.00. If you spend less, the insurance company's obligation is for the lesser of the replacement cost value or the actual amount spent. So instead of getting a check for $320.00, you get a check for $195.00.

Congratulations! By buying this item on sale, you just saved the insurance company $125.00. If you understand how this works up front, you are enabled to make better buying decisions. Maybe, now understanding how this replacement cost system works, you might decide to buy a slightly better or different model. Most insurance companies do not care which model of TV you buy as a replacement. They only care that you purchased a similar TV and that you spent the full agreed replacement cost on this replacement TV.

Assume that your damaged television was a Sony 55-inch set. Let's assume that Best Buy does not have a Sony 55 inch set, but has a Sony 60-inch TV on sale for $850.00. If you decide to go this route, you will need to kick in the $50.00 difference yourself, but in the end you will have maximized the benefits of your policy and for a small addition investment, you have a much nicer replacement TV. If you are happy with the cheaper replacement TV, that is your choice, but at least it is a conscience decision.

We suggest that you go through the entire list of total loss property and highlight those items that you need to replace first and those items with the largest depreciation holdback values make a plan for replacing these items in your first wave of replacements and while you have the ACV insurance check in hand. Do not give the insurer your original receipts; provide them with copies of these receipts. If they insist on obtaining the original receipts, offer in writing, for them to come over to your home and let them look at any receipt they like and allow them to make copies, but we recommend that you not allow them to take possession of them as all too often policyholders never get them back. You may need these receipts for warranty claims if the product fails within the store's replacement policy or for proof of purchase for product warranty repairs.

We are often asked by our clients if they can substitute one item for another, for instance let's say you had a sofa and loveseat set in your home, but you want to go back with a sofa and a recliner chair. This substitution would qualify for recovery of the depreciation holdback money that was set aside by your insurer, because this replacement, while not exactly the same items serve the same function that the lost items served. The same types of substitutions can be made with the replacement of movies on VHS tapes with movies on Blu-ray discs. The policy requires that you replace items of like kind and quality for similar use so as long as you do not stray too far from the original property, the insurer should honor the replacement and issue payment.

The insurer is holding your money and most policies have time limits on making claim for these depreciation holdback benefits. Be certain to get a full and complete copy of your policy and have the adjuster highlight the areas that affect your recovery of the policy benefits. Pay close attention to time limits on submitting for depreciation holdback monies.

But do not give up on recovering the holdback money if there are extenuating circumstances that prevented you from completing the replacements within the policy's allotted time period. Many states have laws that prevent insurance companies from strictly applying the policy's "forfeiture" language when their own acts have prevented the timely replacement of property. In other words, if you have one year to submit your receipts for replacement, but the insurance company took 9 months to settle your claim, many courts will "toll" the period for replacement by the amount of time consumed in the settlement process. Check with an attorney on this issue for the laws in your jurisdiction.

The insurance company will be looking for any excuse to not pay this holdback money to you and even when they do pay, do not expect a check immediately. We often see clients waiting for weeks and even months to get their depreciation holdback money. Remember, the entire insurance system is designed to delay their claim payments and to discourage you from making claim for all of your benefits. The harder they make the process, the better for them because it is a fact that many people will just give up rather than be persistent. And by requiring policyholders to jump through all of these hoops to get the full policy benefits, they know many people will not play this game and will settle for just the actual cash value payment.

Building Property Example

In this example, let's assume that you have settled your insurance claim for fire damage to your commercial building for $250,000.00 at replacement cost value and with a $165,000.00 actual cash value. The insurer is holding $85,000.00 of your money and they are looking at any excuse to not pay this money to you. It is human nature to try to get the best deal on something. No one wants to pay the highest price for an item; we all want to buy it "below wholesale."

So you make a deal to have your brother-in-law, who works in construction, make the repairs on your building. The same requirements for collecting your depreciation holdback on your personal property apply to getting the depreciation holdback payment on the building damages. You must prove that you spent the full replacement cost value to obtain the full amount of depreciation holdback.

An insurance policy is not designed to put money in your pocket; it is designed to collect more in policy premiums than are paid out in claim payments. So in your veal to get the best price from your contractor or to save money on the construction, you must keep in mind that paying less may mean getting less indemnity from your insurance company. Most insurers do not care as much about how you spend the money, but that you spent it and made the repairs they paid for. This does give you some flexibility as you negotiate with contractors for your restoration project.

If you can get the contractor to through in a few extras or upgrades to flooring or cabinets to get your contract, all the better for you and this is the area that can provide you the best value for your money. But, be very careful when contracting for these repairs. Be sure that the contract specifies the full replacement cost value that has been agreed upon with the insurance company. And be certain that the final payment to the contractor is predicated upon your receipt of this indemnity from the insurance company. Insurance companies can be extremely slow in their payment of depreciation holdback monies, often taking weeks or even months to remit a check. Do not place yourself in a default situation with your contractor on the final payment under the contract. Be certain that you and the contractor are both on the same page on payments under his restoration contract.

10. Use the policies benefits to obtain suitable and equivalent temporary housing

Many insurers and their agents try to limit their liability for additional living expense benefits by either not informing consumers of their rights to this coverage at all or by encouraging them to move into a substantially smaller temporary home or maybe an apartment. They often reason that it is only temporary, and most consumers are also under the impression that their relocation will only be temporary and they are willing to tolerate a smaller residence for a short period of time. But, what happens when your stay becomes much longer than expected? Agreeing to move into a house or apartment that is far smaller and has less amenities than your damaged home had only saves the insurance company money. We often hear our consumers tell us that they accepted a much cheaper temporary home, because they wanted to be fair to the insurance company and save them money. They are usually surprised when their efforts to be courteous to the insurer are not reciprocated by a full and fair settlement of their claim.

Moving into a home that does not have the swimming pool your home has or the extra bedrooms for guests that yours has, does not win any favor from insurance companies. All it does is make you less comfortable in these temporary circumstances than you would be if you rented a comparable property to your own. And, there is another possibly unforeseen benefit to insisting upon comparable temporary housing; that being the cost of providing these benefits to the insurance company.

Let's assume that after weeks of negotiations, you reach an impasse with your insurer on the cost of repairing your home. The monthly cost of your temporary housing can be an advantage to getting this difference settled. Assume that the difference between you and the insurance company on your home's damages is $30,000 and your temporary housing costs are $7,000 per month. If you were to demand appraisal, the time it will take to complete the appraisal process, usually at least three months and possibly more, will cost the insurance company an additional $21,000, plus whatever additional amounts you recover in the appraisal process. This places you on more equal ground to negotiate a reasonable compromise resolution of your claim.

Hence, the benefits of insisting upon comparable temporary housing are that you are more comfortable should you need to stay longer than expected and it gives the insurance company a greater incentive to settle your loss and get you back into your home quickly.

Also, do not let yourself be suckered into taking less in the form of amenities either. If your home had 3 televisions, the insurance company owes you for three rental televisions in the temporary home. If your home has a garage, you are entitled to a temporary home with a garage. If you have a swimming pool, they owe you for a temporary home with a pool. If the only available homes have amenities that you home did not have, then they owe you one of these homes as temporary housing.

They also must rent furnishings and a complete housewares package with pots and pans and towels and dishes, etc. The policy owes for the increased cost of maintaining your "normal standard of living" which is generally viewed as a home of similar size and amenities and as close as possible to your home neighborhood. They cannot make you drive all the way across town to save themselves money on your temporary housing claim.

There are so many pitfalls to avoid in the handling of a large loss property claim, it is simply impossible to cover everything here. However, if you follow the above steps you will have at least set the stage for a successful outcome of your claim. Be diligent in your record keeping and documentation, so that hopefully you will never need it. And most importantly, confirm everything in writing to your adjuster; it is amazing what short memories they can have. If it is in writing, you have a record of events that you can use to get what was promised.

APPENDIX II

Choosing a Public Adjuster

Experiencing catastrophic damage to your home or business is can be highly disruptive and traumatic. The decisions you make early in the claim process can have a profound effect on not only your ultimate recovery, but on your mental well-being. Choosing the right Public Adjuster to represent you in the settlement of your insurance claim is a very important decision. Choosing the right adjuster will provide clarity to the process, enable you to focus on your business or family and significantly impact your recovery from the loss. Choosing the wrong Public Adjuster can make an already dreadful situation a nightmare.

Not all Public Adjusters are created equal. Public Adjusters are no different than any other profession; there are both good and bad practitioners. Regrettably, when it comes to Public Adjusters, there are probably more bad ones than good ones. The reason for this is because there is no real school to train Public Adjusters. Many sole proprietor, Public Adjusters start their careers working for insurance companies and learned to handle claims from them. Unfortunately, the business of representing the consumer is very different from representing the interests of an insurance company. For one thing, insurance companies have claims managers overseeing the adjuster's work and scores of attorneys to provide legal guidance when a difficult coverage question arises. Also, very few Public Adjusters have the opportunity to learn the consumer side of adjusting under the guidance of a competent mentor. Add to this the fact that nearly anyone with reasonable intelligence can pass the state Public Adjuster licensing exams with just a few days of study and you have created a system that is designed to produce many poorly trained and/or unqualified Public Adjusters.

Many states have enacted continuing education requirements, which is a step in the right direction, but these requirements come after these new adjusters are already licensed. Until they really know what they are doing, do you want them handling your claim? You have heard the saying "Knowledge is power." When it comes to the business of public adjusting, this phrase could not be more insightful.

The fact is that some public adjusters are better qualified than others. Some demonstrate higher levels of professional integrity. Some have more experience in handling certain types of claims. The key is to find the right adjuster with the right qualifications for your loss situation. Finding the right public adjuster requires a little of your time, but the cost of not properly vetting your chosen public adjuster can be so astronomical that the time invested is a small price to pay for the peace of mind of knowing that you have a true professional protecting your interests.

So how do you go about finding a professional instead of a pretender? To start with, do not rush into a decision on representation and especially do not hire the first Public Adjuster that shows up at your door after a loss. While he may ultimately prove to be the best qualified and the best choice for representation, you cannot possibly know that yet. You need to take some time to research his credentials and references. The following information will help you to choose the right Public Adjuster.

- Request his professional resume. After all, he is applying for a job, to be your claim representative so it is completely reasonable to request his Curriculum vitae. If he cannot produce one or is apprehensive to, do not hire him.

- Verify his formal and insurance specific education. Confirm his claims handling experience. This information should be on his resume and is easily verified by asking for a diploma or contacting the educator's he references.

- Meet personally with the adjuster who will be assigned to handle your claim. Some of the bigger firms send out charming solicitors to secure business, but you could end up with an adjuster who you do not care for. Do not hire a company without first meeting the adjuster assigned to handle your claim.

- Confirm that he will handle your claim in accordance with the steps that have been outlined in Appendix I. Handling claims in this manner takes a great deal more time, which is why many adjusters take short cuts in their claims handling, But following these steps is the only way to professionally handle an insurance claim. Documentation is critical. Get a commitment that he will create a written record of every claim event.

- Develop a list of questions you might have about your claim and ask how he intends to handle your claim. Also, ask him about other similar claims he has handled.

- Verify his business address and telephone number. Some Public Adjusters work out of the trunk of their cars and receive their mail at a mailbox store. If your claim develops problems, it may be difficult to find this guy when you need him most. It is generally better to work with legitimate firm that has a real office and a staff to assist you when your adjuster is busy on another claim or otherwise out of touch.

- Ask for his list of current references and call them. Ask them questions about how this Public Adjuster handled their claim and on how attentive he was in communicating to them throughout the claim process. Be aware that most Public Adjusters will load their references with their best references, so ask for a couple references to clients whose claims did not go smoothly.

- Check with the Department of Insurance to verify that his license and his firm's license are active and in good standing.

- Ask him to produce evidence of Errors and Omissions insurance coverage. This protects you if he makes a major mistake in the handling of your claim that causes a forfeiture of policy benefits. If he does not have this insurance, do not hire him.

- Ask him to produce evidence of workmen's compensation insurance. This protects you if he falls off your roof or is otherwise injured on your property. If he does not have this, do not hire him.

- Ask him to produce evidence of business liability insurance. This insurance can provide you other protections should a situation arise from his claim handling activities. If he does not have this insurance, do not hire him.

- Check consumer organizations such as the BBB (Better Business Bureau) for their records on the firm and their complaint history. Keep in mind that even the best Public Adjuster will occasionally have an unhappy client if they have been in business for any length of time. If the complaint is closed satisfactory, then it is probably not a big deal. However, if he has a history of multiple unresolved complaints, this should be a warning sign to stay away.

- Interview more than one Public Adjuster. You will find that their qualifications may vary and there is the personal element to representation, as this is someone you must work closely with over the next few months. Find someone you get along with and who is attentive to your needs. Of course, remember this is not a popularity contest, so keep that in mind too, but personalities make a difference when working closely.

- Discuss the fees that will be charged. Keep in mind that the lowest fee does not always result in more money in your pocket. A highly qualified professional may charge a higher fee, but if he greatly increases the total recovery, this could result in a much better bargain than the guy with the cheaper fee who did not increase the value of the claim settlement. Beware of the solicitors who attempt to sell you their services by telling you they will beat everyone's lowest fee to get your business. These types generally do not add value to your claim but rely upon taking their fees off the top of the insurance company's settlement offer and do little work to increase your recovery. Don't be fooled by the size of the company. Some of the largest and oldest public adjusting companies in the country have been known to practice public adjusting in this manner.

- Look at the adjuster's professional affiliations. Memberships in nationally recognized or regional adjusting groups show that he is probably serious about continuing education and professionalism. Look for membership in organizations like NAPIA (National Public Insurance Adjuster Association), TAPIA (Texas Public Insurance Adjuster Association), RMAPIA (Rocky Mountain Association of Public Insurance Adjusters) or FAPIA (Florida Association of Public Insurance Adjusters). Even more importantly, look for individuals that maintain membership in professional insurance education associations, as these are the adjusters who are truly committed to professional insurance education; groups like the SCLA (Society of Claims Law Associates), CPCU (Chartered Property Casualty Underwriters Society), the Institute's Associate in Claims (AIC) is another popular designation as is the newly developed (SPPA) Senior Professional Public Adjuster designation. Also, the CLM (Claims and Litigation Management Alliance). These organizations offer professional designations for completion of insurance education programs and hold in-depth continuing education programs. Regrettably, very few public adjusters engage in this type of intensive continuing insurance education.

Timing of Hiring a Public Adjuster

When is the best time to retain a public adjuster? This depends upon the size and complexity of your claim and to a lesser degree the luck of the draw with respect to the adjuster assigned to your claim. We are occasionally and pleasantly surprised to find a competent professional company adjuster on the other side of a claim. Regrettably, this is by far the exception rather than the rule in today's claims environment. That being said, there is occasionally a claim situation that does not require professional representation. We recently had a claim like this in Texas, where the loss was well in excess of the policy's coverage, so there was no need for our services. Similarly, we recently had a claim in Illinois on a total fire loss to a grocery store. On this claim, the adjuster just after we were hired agreed to pay the policy limits, so we voluntarily[30] modified our contract and took only a percentage of any new recoveries we achieved. In this case, we were able to use several of the 'Additional Coverages provisions" of the policy to increase his settlement by an additional $42,000, plus a sizable recovery for his loss of business income.

You should not be in a rush to hire anyone, but our experience shows that having your claim representative in place early in the claim process is preferable for a large or complex loss. An experienced adjuster can help you to make decisions that are the most beneficial to you and which may not be the decisions that the company's adjuster will suggest. A Public Adjuster is not concerned with insurance company's profits, but in helping you to get into a more stable and suitable situation so that you can focus on your family or your business during the recovery process.

A Public Adjuster can present you options that often are often not communicated by the insurance company's adjuster; options like using the policy's extra expense coverage to establish a temporary business location or purchasing products from a competitor to fill your customer's current orders so that you don't lose their business permanently. A good Public Adjuster can often use certain policy provisions to protect the business' financial future from losses long after the business is restored. Insurance companies don't really care what happens after the business is restored and they are off the hook for payments under the policy, so they may not advise or encourage these types of extra expense expenditures.

We are often contacted weeks and months after a loss, when a claim has become a huge problem, to assist in correcting the situation. It is important to recognize that some prior actions or decisions cannot be undone and they can significantly impact your claim recovery. It is a fine line between being too quick to hire representation and too late. We cannot help you know where this line is drawn, as each claim is as unique as a fingerprint.

Public Adjuster Representation Typically Resulted In Larger Payments to Policyholders

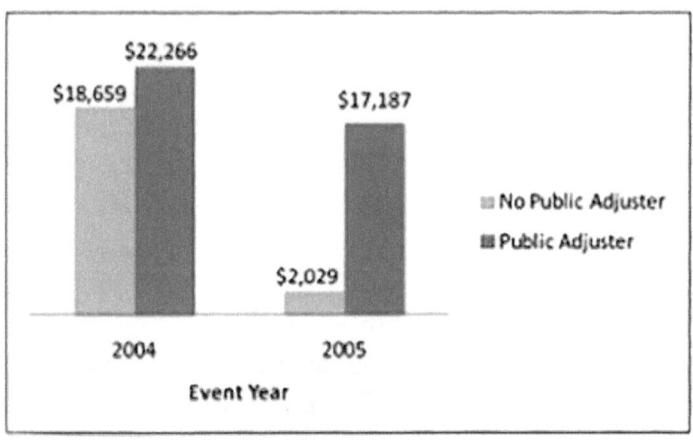

Source: OPPAGA analysis. Data refers to the median (50th percentile or typical) payment.

APPENDIX III

Choosing an Attorney

Just as with Public Adjusters, attorney qualifications can also vary drastically. While an attorney with a law license can legally represent you in a claim situation, not every attorney is intimately familiar with insurance claims handling and few have the litigation experience necessary to take on and defeat the insurance companies' legions of defense attorneys. It is rare indeed to have an experienced bad faith attorney willing to engage in the processing of a claim. Just as you would not go to a podiatrist for brain surgery, having an attorney who does not routinely work in insurance bad faith litigation is a recipe for disaster. Some of the worst situations we have experienced with our clients were the result of the retention of an attorney who was unfamiliar with insurance bad faith litigation. Not long ago, we had a client who hired his old college buddy who had gone on to law school after college. His friend was going to help him out with his claim situation and sue the insurance company for bad faith, but in the end he got very poor results and it was clear to us that he did not know how to create value to get a good settlement. This is not how you want to choose your legal counsel.

The quickest way to find attorneys familiar with insurance bad faith is to ask several public adjusters for referrals. Most public adjusters work routinely with bad faith attorneys and are more than happy to provide a reference. Get recommendations from several public adjusters, because most have one or two attorneys whom they favor, possibly for reasons other than their legal abilities. We generally recommend two or three attorneys when it is time to litigate a claim matter, because personalities matter when you are going down the 1 to 2 year road of litigation. Finding someone who is the right fit is important.

Like public adjusters, many insurance bad faith attorneys are lazy. They want to push for a quick claim settlement that requires them to do the least amount of work. Some of our biggest frustrations are with attorneys who our clients have chosen, without our input and three months into the litigation process, they call up and tell us that they have settled the case in mediation. We know that three months is not enough time to have completed any reasonable discovery, so essentially they have sold the claim out for a quick easy fee and have convinced the consumer that this is really the best deal for them. We have had some very good litigations destroyed like this and it is extremely frustrating when we put so much hard work into thoroughly documenting the insurance company's wrongful actions and behavior, only to achieve nickels on the dollar in the claim resolution.

To protect yourself, do your research. Find an attorney with a reputation for aggressiveness and with a history of large insurance recoveries. Find an attorney who has engaged in a reasonable number of insurance bad faith trials. Many attorneys who practice in insurance bad faith, have not seen the inside of a courtroom in years. We have met attorneys who we believe were intimidated by the idea of trying a case. Find an attorney who does insurance bad faith litigation, as the focus of their practice. These attorneys have developed intimate knowledge of insurance company processes and know how to create value for your case, through targeted discovery requests and through tactfully filing motions to compel discovery and to limit their defenses. To put it another way, they know "where the bodies are buried," so they know how to get to the insurance company's Achilles heel. Remember that insurance companies are expert in evaluating risk. When your attorney has created enough risk for them, they will be more motivated to settle with you closer to your terms than theirs. It takes a tremendous amount of work and knowledge of the insurance litigation process to get to this point.

Author's Note

The conduct described in this book is not an indictment of every insurance company or every adjuster or the processing of all claims. While the problems with claims handling are becoming epidemic, there are still a handful of good insurance companies and still many good and ethical company and independent adjusters working to fulfill the insurer's promise of coverage.

Unfortunately, these folks are becoming fewer and farther between, as they reach retirement and are replaced with ambitious young adjusters who have been indoctrinated into the insurance companies' new profit focused mindset. We know of many of these "old Pros" who are biding their time until they reach retirement age. Many have spoken privately to us on the changes the claims industry has seen over the last ten years and most are glad to be getting out. Others simply roll their eyes to us at site inspections, more or less admitting their understanding of the inappropriateness of the claim position they are being forced to pursue, while acknowledging their inability to do anything about it.

With this in mind, we want to pay tribute here to the many true claims professionals with whom we deal with on a daily basis. We know who you are and we respect you.

Endnotes

1. *Rawlings v. Apodaca*, 151 Ariz. 149; 726 P.2d 565 (1986)
2. *Campbell v. State Farm*, 538 U.S. 408; 123 S. Ct. 1513; 155 L. Ed. 2d 585; (2003)
3. *Hawkins v. Allstate*, 152 Ariz. 490; 733 P.2d 1073; (1987)
4. Bloomberg Magazine September 2007
5. Consumer Reports May 2014
6. Bloomberg Report September 2007
7. www.theguardian.com/business/2002/mar/24/enron.theobserver
8. www.propertycasualty360.com/2008/04/07/allstate-releases-entire-mckinsey-report-for-review
9. From the McKinsey/Allstate Documents
10. Good Hands To Boxing Gloves,
11. www.accenture.com/us-en/Pages/service-insurance-claims-components...
12. Note: Not all states require Disclosure Statements
13. *Zuckerman vs. Transamerica Ins. Co.*, 650 P.2d 441 (Ariz. 1982)
14. *Gilderman v. State Farm Ins.*, 649 A.2d 941 (Pa. Super. 1994)
15. *Salesin v. State Farm Fire & Cas.*, 581 N.W.2d 781 (Mich. Ct. App. 1998)
16. Claims Magazine August 2000
17. *Tritschler v. Allstate*, 144 P.3d 519 (Ariz. App. 2006)
18. *Trinidad v. Florida Peninsula Insurance Co.*, 99 So. 3d 502, 504 (Fla. 3d DCA 2011)
19. Remodeling November 2013
20. Consumer Reports May 2014
21. From actual estimates prepared on Xactware estimating software
22. Property Loss Adjusting by James Markham
23. Insurance Journal May 30, 2006
24. The Washington Post Sisters Blew Whistle on Katrina Claims By MICHAEL KUNZELMAN The Associated Press Saturday, August 26, 2006; 8:36 PM
25. *State Farm Lloyds v. Nicolau*, 951 S.W.2d 444 (Tex. 1997)
26. *All Saints Catholic Church v. United National Insurance Company*, 257 S.W.3d 800
27. *Cedar Bluff Townhome Condo. Ass'n v. American Family Mut. Ins. Co.*, (Citation unknown)
28. Wikipedia (http://en.wikipedia.org/wiki/History_of_insurance)
29. Property Casualty Insurers Association of America (http://www.pciaa.net/pciwebsite/Cms/Content/ViewPage?sitePageId=37458)
30. Some states have regulations that prevent the charging of fees in these situations. In this case the law was silent, but integrity wasn't.